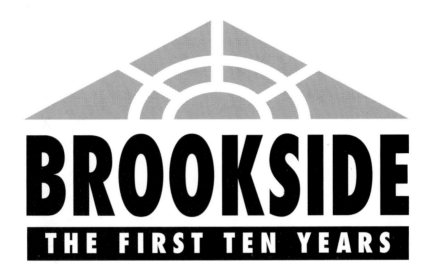

BROOKSIDE

THE FIRST TEN YEARS

PHIL REDMOND'S
BROOKSIDE
THE FIRST TEN YEARS

BY

GEOFF TIBBALLS

A CHANNEL 4 BOOK

ACKNOWLEDGEMENTS

The author would like to thank the following for their kind
assistance in the preparation of this book: Phil Redmond,
Mal Young, Philip Reevell, Janice Troup, Simone Sless,
staff and the cast of *Brookside* at Mersey Television,
Jane Friggens at Channel Four, and editor
Krystyna Zukowska at Boxtree.

First published in 1992 by
Boxtree Limited
21 Broadwall
London SE1 9PL

Text © 1992 Phil Redmond Enterprises
Illustrations © 1992 Mersey TV
13579108642

Designed and typeset by axis design
Printed and bound by OFSA, Spa, Italy

A CIP catalogue for this book is available from the British
Library

ISBN 1 85283 197 9

The publishers would like to thank Anne Johnson for copyediting the text,
Sven Arnstein for the front cover photograph, and Trevor Owens for many of
the photographs used inside this book.

CONTENTS

FOREWORD

Phil Redmond.

When *Brookside* started in 1982, people used to say to me: 'It's different from other soaps — it's more real, it's like the news or a football match.'

That was exactly the sort of reaction I wanted to hear. I wanted *Brookside* to be different — to break the mould if you like — but above all to be realistic. I just wanted to show life as it is. For I see *Brookside* as being about modern Britain, about real people.

There are two ways in which we have achieved this authenticity — through the look of the programme and through its content. The key to obtaining the right look was the decision to buy the six houses that now make up *Brookside* Close. These are real bricks and mortar. There are none of the wobbly walls and bannisters that you find in studio sets. Each house has its own character and this, plus the fact that all of the shooting is done on location, all serves to enhance the air of reality. Last year, we added the parade of shops — again these are genuine buildings. Within these settings, we have made important strides too. In the early days, I won the right to use realistic props. Until then, people had spent hours blanking out things like labels on sauce bottles and I thought this was an insult to the audience's intelligence.

The other respect in which *Brookside* was different was that we used a single camera instead of the usual multi-camera system. This is why viewers liken it to the news because we use the same ENG cameras that they do on the news. People see our electronic image on screen and make the connection that it is reality.

I set out to reflect Britain as it

was in the 1980s and so the setting was vital. For one thing, I didn't want a pub. I was fed up watching dramas where people wandered into a pub and spilled out all their intimate life details — you know, 'A pint of Guinness, please — and have you heard about my prostate operation?' Nobody does that. Also I thought that the concept of a pub on every corner was so dated. It was all fun pubs at the time and kids would never be seen dead in the same pub as their Mums and Dads. In the late seventies and early eighties, the whole country seemed to be under the bulldozer and the old communities were being destroyed. It was all new estates — people no longer popped next door to borrow a cup of sugar. In winter, neighbours would never even see each other.

I was interested in all this and so I came up with a mix of characters from different socio-economic groups living next door to one another on a mixed estate. There were people who would be on the way up, people who would be on the way down; shop-floor, middle-management and professional people; the black economy, trade unionists and Conservatives. What I did was juxtapose them. So we would have an issue such as unemployment running through the show, but instead of having our characters arguing over a table in the same room, we would cut from scene to scene and have different discussions on the same topic. So the Grants and the Collinses would give their different viewpoints and it was up to the audience to take from this what they wanted.

The idea was that we wouldn't be lecturing, although there have been times over the ten years when I'll admit that we have jumped on our soap box and given the audience a really hard time. I remember an episode with Sandra, the nurse, who changed a patient's bed and ended up giving her an eight-minute lecture on the problems of the National Health Service. I watched it on transmission and thought: 'How did I let that go through?'

What we've done is put flesh and blood people into real houses — not just cardboard cut-outs into cardboard sets. The aim has always been to feature stories and human beings that you recognise and know — the type of people with whom you can identify. Each character in *Brookside* is a human being with an imperfect but very real personality. Our viewers watch a character dealing with his or her life and they can relate to similar events in their own lives. *Brookside*'s strength is that it takes issues and shows their impact on real people.

So the characters I came up with were characters who could reflect and symbolise the great debates that were running through society. And now when we do our three- and five-year re-vamps, this is the principle to which we go back, and we ask ourselves: 'Which section of society have we left out or is under-represented?' Recently, we introduced the Harrisons with a strong middle-class ethic. He has been part of the enterprise culture and has retired early, she is in education. And education is going to be the big debate of the nineties.

School has always been important to *Brookside* because at that age it's woven into your life. So the school has always featured strongly — even back in the days of Damon Grant. Another first for us was that we treated youngsters as central characters in an adult drama — not just as walk-ons or unseen offspring who spent six months of the year upstairs. Damon and Karen Grant were given as much time on screen as their parents Sheila and Bobby,

Ron Dixon carries DD over the threshold of the Trading Post to mark the opening of the Brookside parade of shops.

simply because they were people in their own right. I've found that if you write about teenagers, not only do you get teenagers watching but you get older people watching, too. This is because it's nostalgic. And nostalgia starts yesterday.

The young actors that we get on *Brookside* are natural. They haven't all been to stage school. That was something I learned on *Grange Hill* — that kids might be able to sing and tap dance but it doesn't mean they can ride a bike with no hands. I remember writing a scene for *Grange Hill* in which a lad had to balance a broom on his forehead and the actor in question couldn't do it. That's why we got kids from comprehensive schools. And it's the same with *Brookside*. With some characters, you need to have had a bit more professional training but with others you just want an empathy, an understanding. We tend not to use established actors. I believe that when someone appears on screen, the first thing the viewers should be interested in is the character. They shouldn't get into a guessing game as to where they've seen him or her

before, because while they're doing that, they could actually have lost what we're trying to tell them.

Looking back over the ten years, I wanted to break new ground, and I think we've done that. We've led the way in tackling major issues such as rape, drug abuse and unemployment. I think it's fair to say that without the existence of *Brookside*, *EastEnders* would not be the show it is today. It would probably have been much softer — more like *Coronation Street*. Not only have we changed the content of television soap operas but we've changed the shooting style, too. The BBC built its lot for *EastEnders*, and *Coronation Street* has been forced to get out of the studio more. At the same time, we've had to become a little more mainstream as the years have gone on.

Brookside should now be safe for another ten years. All our hard work over the past year or so has been an investment for the next ten. *Brookside* needs to stay. One of the reasons we expanded from two to three nights a week was that Channel Four was going to be selling its own advertising from 1993 and, with *Brookside* being its flagship drama, twice a week was not going to be a big enough psychological commitment for the audience to make. Obviously, a highly-rated drama serial will become all the more important to the commercial future of the channel.

We could actually do five nights a week but we settled on three as a compromise. If we had done five nights, we would have had to change to multi-camera techniques. Even so, just because we've shot *Brookside* single camera for ten years doesn't mean we can't move to a multi-camera format. Technology is so advanced these days that they wouldn't have to be the big dinosaur cameras of the studios.

Content-wise, the next ten years

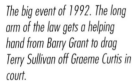

The big event of 1992. The long arm of the law gets a helping hand from Barry Grant to drag Terry Sullivan off Graeme Curtis in court.

have got to be spent re-visiting the issues that we've covered over the previous ten. A lot of the issues that we concentrate on will never go away. One of television's biggest problems is the 'we've done that' syndrome, and that's why I constantly come back to themes like drugs, alcohol abuse, dyslexia and illiteracy. They've been around since time immemorial and they don't go away just because *Brookside* has covered them. I think the job of innovation is not only to deal with new themes but also to re-visit old ones with a new interpretation. That's the challenge for the next ten years.

We have to reflect the changing society of the nineties. We've been through the strident eighties, what we're into now is the subtle nineties, where the marketing sell has got to be slightly softer because the audience are a bit fed up with the harsh, kitchen-sink soap-box message. They say, 'We know all that,' so you have to put a different perspective on the whole thing. That's the challenge of doing a long-running serial — it's always the same but it's always different.

Our role, too, is not to let the Independent Television Commission become cosy. Every now and again our job is to shake the cage. I know at the end of the day that's what the public expect from us. They want *Brookside* to be challenging. And it will continue to be.

1 MEET THE BOSS

'I got into writing as a negative reaction to what I was doing. I was fed up with counting bags of cement and grit as a quantity surveyor. It wasn't hard.'

So says Phil Redmond who, within ten years of packing in his day job in 1972, had become one of the most influential men in British television. He had devised the award-winning *Grange Hill* for the BBC and had formed his own production company, Mersey Television, to produce another of his innovative creations, *Brookside*, for Channel Four.

Phil Redmond is the archetypal local boy made good. Born in 1949 on a council estate in Huyton, Harold Wilson's old constituency just to the east of Liverpool, he passed his 11-plus before succumbing to the vagaries of the education system. 'I was sent to a comprehensive school in Liverpool as part of the great social experiment of the 1960s — in fact I was one of the first two per cent to go through the comprehensive system. The classes were far too big and the result was that, after seven years, I left school with one 'A' Level and four 'O' Levels. I should have left with five 'A' Levels and ten 'O' Levels.

'On leaving school, I went into quantity surveying. With hindsight, I should have gone into architecture because instead of totting up bags of cement, I probably should have been designing the buildings. I did quantity surveying for five years but I felt there must be more to life than this. The only other thing I'd ever done was write comedy sketches with a guy at school so I gave up my surveying job to go on the dole and see if I could write.

'I gave it six months and nothing happened, except that I sold one comedy sketch to Harry Secombe for a series he was doing with Yorkshire Television. I decided to give myself another three months and, on the Thursday before I was due to go back to being a quantity surveyor, Producer Humphrey Barclay phoned me from London Weekend Television to say that he was buying one of my ideas for *Doctor In Charge*. Suddenly I found myself writing alongside the likes of John Cleese, Graeme Garden and Bill Oddie.'

This was just the break Phil needed. Further commissions followed, including episodes for two ATV series — the office comedy *The Squirrels*, which starred Bernard Hepton and Ken Jones, and the children's adventure *Kids From 47A*.

'But mixing with people in television had given me a bit of an inferiority complex because everyone in TV seemed to have been educated at Oxford or Cambridge. So I decided to go and do a degree in social studies as a mature student at Liverpool University. I knew by then what I wanted to do with my life — and that was to write — and during the second year of my course I thought up the idea of doing a realistic drama about schools, as opposed to the sort of Enid Blyton Boys' Own adventures that there had always been on TV.

'I wanted to make it for kids from my type of background — something that they could identify with. Having worked with ITV, I tried to sell the notion to the various ITV companies but none of them was interested, although ATV did produce a rather similar series called *Bunch of Fives*. But that didn't last long. By then, I had managed to get the BBC interested and in 1976

Grange Hill was born. Today, 16 years later, ITV would love to have *Grange Hill*!'

The relationship between Phil Redmond and the BBC was, to say the least, somewhat strained. 'I found myself arguing with the BBC hierarchy about the integrity of the programme. They were people roughly my age but who had the power of veto over my script. I started to realise that all these arguments are merely about opinions, and that the opinion that matters is the one held by the person with power. It doesn't matter whether they're right or not.

'My other experience was trying to develop a programme called *County Hall* with the BBC. I wanted it to be twice a week and about county politics. I did some research in Liverpool and London and, funnily enough, four years ago when I was moving office and transferring a load of archive boxes, I opened up a *County Hall* research file from 1979. On the top of this file was a note saying: "These are the two people to watch in the 1980s — Ken Livingstone and Derek Hatton..."

'I remember going to the GLC one day and sitting in the Council chamber. It was really stuffy and boring until suddenly this guy arrived in jeans and leather jacket. It was as if he'd kicked the door in — he hadn't, but his entry had the same effect. Everyone started to mumble and he casually sat down and put his feet up on the table. It was Ken Livingstone.

'Anyway, *County Hall* got pushed through but the BBC appointed a Producer without telling me, and then they cut the series length from 26 episodes to 13, also without telling me. The Producer they'd appointed didn't understand county politics and wanted to turn the subject matter into borough politics, about town halls. We had no end of ding-dongs, culminating in a huge row in the office of the then Head of Series at the BBC, David Reid. This Producer said that if I stayed on the project, he'd go. David Reid pointed out that it was, after all, my project and so the Producer went. For the first time in its history, the BBC put a programme into production without a Producer.

'*County Hall* eventually went out on BBC2 after the BBC had made a resource decision that instead of making one project, they'd make two. But being classically BBC, what they did was just chop the budget in half — the other series was Ted Whitehead's *World's End*

Sheila Grant (Sue Johnston) enriched her life by teaching at a deaf school.

about a pub in Chelsea. So both projects were under-resourced. *County Hall* went out at 7pm. I've looked at all the tapes and actually it wasn't bad. We got a couple of million viewers on BBC2 and then, at the end of the 13, it came off. So did *World's End*.

'At the same time, I'd been developing a teenage series called *Going Out* for Southern Television. Everything that could go right with a programme went right with *Going Out* — the budget was fine, the Director was great — but everything that could go wrong went wrong with *County Hall*. I learned a lot from comparing the two experiences.

'I realised all this time that what was building up inside me was the quest for creative control. When Channel Four arrived, that was my opportunity. Being a good Merseysider, I realised the only way to do it was to take the Marxist ethic of seizing the means of production and set up as an independent Producer, because I wanted to be the one who decided how the budget was spent — whether it went on more actors, locations, or whatever.'

And so Mersey Television was formed to make *Brookside*. The rest, as they say, is history.

As the boss, Phil Redmond is not allowed to have any favourite *Brookside* characters, nor does he lose any sleep at night about killing off members of the cast. 'I've never worried about killing off stars — I work on the basis that the programme was there before the cast. If an actor or an actress wants to leave the show, that's fine because the

Radio City disc jockey Peter Price (right) celebrates a special Christmas edition of his show from Brookside *with Producer Mal Young, Michael Starke (Sinbad), Cheryl Maiker (Marcia) and Louis Emerick (Mick).*

estate setting is transitory — people do move in and out. In fact, I think we were very fortunate to keep Amanda Burton, who played Heather, and Sue Johnston, who played Sheila, for as long as we did. Mandy stayed for five years and Sue for seven — and that's a long time on any series.

'Seeing that first episode of *Brookside* on screen was obviously a big moment for me and I think getting through the first year was a major achievement. After 90 episodes, I reckon we'd just about got it right so I would say that the end of that first year was my personal golden age of *Brookside*. That was when we had the breakdown of Heather and Roger's marriage and that meant a lot to me personally because I wrote those scripts, too.

They were the last ones I wrote for *Brookside* so I suppose there's also an emotional attachment. But I also think that, after a year, I had finally shown people what I was trying to achieve. Up until then, it was fighting all the time, saying, "I don't want *Coronation Street*, I don't want *Crossroads* — I want this."

'The 1,000th episode in October 1991 was a landmark, too. We had expanded to three times a week by then and I knew that it was going to work, in spite of the press casting doubts about the show's future. So it was a great moment reaching 1,000. I thought then that I could, if I wanted to, actually stop and walk away from it all and nobody could take those 1,000 episodes of *Brookside* away from me.'

As well as being Chairman of Mersey Television and Executive Producer of *Brookside*, Phil Redmond became an Honorary Professor of Media Studies at Liverpool Polytechnic. He was awarded a fellowship in July 1989.

'It's ironic but I am now officially the longest-serving member of Channel Four. I find myself mixing at all levels of the television industry. I go to *Grange Hill* meetings where I have no official status — I'm just the guy who came up with the idea; at Mersey Television I'm the Chairman; I go as guest or as guru in my professorial capacity and sit at debates next to BBC bosses like John Birt; and when I was a bidder for the North-West franchise, I was in with the ITV mob.

'It's easy to look back and think that all my years at comprehensive school and as a quantity surveyor were fruitless. But the comprehensive school gave me the idea for *Grange Hill*, and my knowledge of quantity surveying has been invaluable in making *Brookside* financially viable.

'So nothing is ever wasted... except maybe counting bags of cement.'

2 A SOAP IS BORN

The year was 1980 and the setting was a huge open meeting chaired by Jeremy Isaacs, former Programme Controller of Thames Television and then the founding Chief Executive of the new Channel Four, due to hit the screens two years later. In the midst of the assembled gathering of some of the brightest minds in television, a gaunt, thin Liverpudlian posed a question to Jeremy Isaacs.

'If you want to make programmes on Channel Four that are innovative and different, will you make programmes for teenagers and allow us to say "fuck" at 8 o'clock in the evening?'

The whole room seemed to fall silent. Isaacs turned round to look at the questioner and replied, 'Well, if the context is right...' Then he added: 'Who are you?'

'Phil Redmond,' came the reply.

'Oh, *Grange Hill*,' said Isaacs knowingly. 'Come and see me in my office after this meeting.'

The idea for a drama serial set among residents on a new housing estate had been in Phil Redmond's mind for seven years. He had submitted an outline to the five major ITV companies and the BBC back in 1973 but all of them had turned it down. In those days, he was just another unknown writer and television can be about as easy to break into as the Bank of England, but by 1981 he had the hugely successful *Grange Hill* on his CV. The impending birth of Channel Four seemed to be the perfect opportunity to realise his dreams.

So Phil Redmond put his suggestion to Jeremy Isaacs and David Rose, the Head of Fiction at Channel Four. 'I said to them: "If you're going to be innovative, you're still going to need to deliver an audience to attract advertising. Every channel has a soap — how about a twice-weekly for Channel Four?"

'Jeremy liked the idea but was

Brookside Close — a haven of peace until the families arrived.

worried about the money. But I said: "I used to be a quantity surveyor and I can show you how, with proper cost management, we can drive the cost right down."

'I said: "What's your cost yardstick?" And he said: "£30,000 an hour."

'I also showed David Rose a couple of *Going Out* cassettes and I later found out that they had taken them to a big Channel Four meeting at which David had announced: "This is the kind of drama that Channel Four should be making." If I'd known that at the time, it would have strengthened my negotiating position.'

Phil went off armed with Jeremy's figures. 'I used the principle that if you invest heavily in the beginning and automate the production process as much as you can, the continuing costs are much lower.' He did his sums and was able to present a package that proved exceedingly attractive to the Channel Four hierarchy. *Brookside* was on its way.

The deciding factor was Phil's idea of buying six houses to form a permanent set. 'At the time, the average set construction cost was £13,000 per half-hour on television and that was to build, store, tear down and destroy the set at the end. It was ridiculous. It didn't take me long to twig that, with the houses on *Brookside* costing £25,000 each, after 13 weeks the whole site would be paid for and after four months the equipment would be paid for too. So that was clearly the way to do it.

'Also, by using the latest technology, we were able to put in a higher production value with the single-camera technique that has produced the *Brookside* look. Another advantage was that every bit of that site was cabled so, at the start of each day's shooting, we simply went in and switched it on. That saved us an hour and a half each day setting up. Anyway, Channel Four agreed to it

THE CAST FOR THAT FIRST WEEK

Bobby Grant	Ricky Tomlinson	**Gizzmo Hawkins**	Robert Smith
Sheila Grant	Sue Johnston	**Ducksie Brown**	Mark Birch
Barry Grant	Paul Usher	**Matty Nolan**	Tony Scoggins
Damon Grant	Simon O'Brien	**Susi**	Helen Murphy
Karen Grant	Shelagh O'Hara	**Pauline**	Jeanette Debs
Heather Huntington	Amanda Burton	**Priest**	Peter Holmes
Roger Huntington	Rob Spendlove	**Griff**	Gary Roberts
Annabelle Collins	Doreen Sloane	**Jacko**	Paul Stanton
Paul Collins	Jim Wiggins	**Fay**	Michelle Edwards
Lucy Collins	Katrin Cartlidge	**Dawn**	Mary Fay

all and off we went. It sounds easy now but in reality it took 18 months.'

So why set the new soap in Liverpool? Phil Redmond explains: 'To meet Channel Four's financial requirements, we couldn't do it in London for two reasons — the rent and labour costs were just too high. Also, I wanted to do something different. You can't sit in a temple and denounce the religion. You have to go to a mountain and shout it out — and the mountain was Merseyside. Besides, that's where I come from and if I was going to spend £4 million a year, as I was then, there was no better place to spend it than Merseyside.'

Another factor behind Phil Redmond's decision to make the new serial on a permanent location set was the effect it would have on the production team. 'Over the years, I'd observed the crews in television studios. They often looked bored — as if they weren't living up to their potential. But on a film set, it was always a totally different atmosphere. I wanted to capture that vibrancy, along with the economy and control of the studios. So I married the two together.'

It was the need for control that prompted Phil to choose a cul de sac for his location. At least that way there was only the need to worry

about sealing off one end from the inquisitive members of the public and stray dogs who can turn filming days into a nightmare.

'Having decided on Liverpool, I met the Chief Executive of the County Council and told him what I wanted to do. He had his men look around and they came up with a few builders who were building large sites. One firm, Broseleys, were re-developing Lord Sefton's estate. When Lord Sefton died in the 1970s, part of the estate was bequeathed to the city on the basis that it remained a working estate. The interpretation was to build 3,000 houses on it and that's where *Brookside* Close is today.

'I met the guys from Broseleys and they showed me the site plans. This one particular cul de sac stood out — it had a brook running next to it, hence the name. It was ideal. It was virgin — they hadn't started on it yet. In fact, it was well away from the main area of building and it took them six years to catch up with us. They were at one end of the site, we were at the other.

'In keeping with my insistence on reality, I gave the builders a list of the programme's characters, together with a short profile of each character, and they said that these types of people would buy these types of houses. So the homes were actually tailored to the characters. Remember that in the eighties the concept of mixed housing was completely new. When I was a quantity surveyor, it was all 250 boxes of the same standard design. But we mixed bungalows and houses (we have one bungalow, number 6, and five houses) and now it's standard practice. But it was a new technique then. And I'm pleased to say that, after ten years, our timber-framed houses have stood up to ten life-times — they're excellent.

'The site was built in four months, from February to June, and all the

Filming at the fateful scaffolding for the downfall of Sue and Daniel.

houses were delivered by crane from the factory. One day, you'd go and it was just the framework, the next day a house would be there!

'We haven't done that much to the houses over the years, apart from widening the odd door or stairway. Mick Johnson's bungalow has sliding double doors leading into the lounge but that wasn't a design fea-

ture. I asked the builders to put in double doors so that we could get a better camera angle and an extra door in his kitchen so that we could shoot both ways. That's now been incorporated in all the builders' future designs — I tried to get a royalty but...'

The first episode of *Brookside* was transmitted at 8pm on 2 November 1982, the inaugural evening of Channel Four. For the record, other Channel Four programmes on that historic day included *The Paul Hogan Show*, Ian McKellen in the *Film On Four*, *Walter*, The Comic Strip's hilarious Enid Blyton spoof, *Five Go Mad In Dorset* and, of course, *Countdown*.

The very first words on *Brookside*

were spoken by a milkman chastising a dog, 'Get out of it. Go on.' The action then cut to the Grants with Bobby calling out, 'Hey, there's a cup of tea on there. Come on.' Incidentally, that same milkman was recalled to speak the opening line of the 1,000th episode.

That initial episode also saw the Collins family waking up on Saturday morning. It was the last morning of their old life in a large detached house on the Wirral before, forced by Paul being made redundant from his job as Production Manager at a local chemical firm, they descended a rung or two on the social ladder and moved into 8 *Brookside* Close. There they encountered the two families already resident on the Close — the Huntingtons (Heather and Roger) and the Grants who, conversely, were moving up in the world from a run-down council estate.

By the mid-eighties, *Brookside* had developed into Channel Four's most popular programme, often towering above other programmes shown on the channel in terms of ratings. When Jeremy Isaacs, who had commissioned the programme in the first place, was succeeded by Michael Grade in 1988, there was a suggestion that *Brookside* should be brought forward to a 6pm time slot in order to capture more teenage viewers. Eventually it was resolved to increase the number of *Brookside* episodes to three per week – a move that took effect from July 1990.

It soon became apparent that, in order to accommodate the third episode, *Brookside* needed to expand. It had to escape from the confines of the Close, where the only regular meeting place for characters was a postbox, and to search for new horizons. Thus *Brookside* Shopping Parade was created and this, together with a greater emphasis on the goings-on at *Brookside* Comprehensive, has shifted the pro-gramme away from the Close, where many of the key issues of the eighties were debated and enacted, to '*Brookside* Community', a society that is living out the dilemmas facing individuals in the nineties.

Of course, it requires more than a new location to keep viewers hooked. The drama on screen had to keep pace with the changes off it. In early 1991, a long-term planning meeting held in the Lake District mapped out the way ahead.

The opening of the new shopping parade was timed for the 1,000th episode on 9 October 1991. The murder of Sue Sullivan was scheduled to create maximum audience interest

WORKING HOLIDAYS

In the past, the only way you knew soap characters had been to, say, Spain was because they sent a postcard from Malaga and came back with a fake sun-tan (newly acquired in make-up) and clutching a straw donkey. But in *Brookside*, you know because you actually see them there.

As a result of the streamlined technology that allows Mersey Television to produce 75 minutes of quality drama a week at a cost that is lower than the average cost per hour of most programmes, *Brookside* has always been able to get out and about and go further afield than Goodison Park or the Mersey Ferry.

Over the years, *Brookside* has been to Benidorm (with Bobby and Sheila Grant), Portugal (Heather Haversham and Tom Curzon), Barbados (Terry Sullivan and Pat Hancock), Rome (Bobby and Sheila Grant again), Austria (Terry Sullivan and Jonathan Gordon-Davies) and Rhodes (Tracy Corkhill and Nikki White) — not to mention less exotic climes such as the Isle of Man, Northern Ireland, Cardiff, Glasgow, Edinburgh, Torquay, Tunbridge Wells and Shrewsbury.

And it's no great logistical exercise, since *Brookside* travels light. The crew just hop in a minibus and off they go. But there were a few anxious faces on the Barbados trip when the tapes sent to record the scenes went missing en route to the airport. Fortunately, they turned up in time.

When Bobby and Sheila went to Rome, special permission was needed to shoot in Vatican City and St. Peter's Square — where they even managed to get

in the days leading up to the 1,000th episode. The return of Owen Daniels and his relationship with Sammy Rogers were to strengthen the growing interest in the programme among teenage viewers.

The social issues that have been the hallmark of *Brookside's* traditional values were to be handled in a more subtle way but would still be there, in the shape of everyday racism experienced by second-generation ethnic minorities, drugs in schools, divorce and broken families, and women's health.

By August, the changes in the drama were working their way into the on-screen action and viewers started to lap up the relationship between Sue Sullivan and Barry Grant. Audience figures rose sharply. *Brookside* had safely entered a new age.

Even so, nobody at *Brookside* ever rests on their laurels. Phil Redmond says: 'I'm always reminding our writers that we're in constant competition. There is always the temptation for viewers to flick channels. So in the first five minutes of each episode, we've got to tell the audience that this show is worth watching.'

On the piste. Terry (Brian Regan) and Jonathan (Steven Pinner) go ski-ing in Austria with Cheryl (Jennifer Calvert).

(Insert) Wish you were here. Nikki White and Tracy Corkhill go for a Greek dip.

the Pope in the background, at his balcony. To ensure that shooting went smoothly, a priest from Liverpool accompanied the crew. It worked so well that the Pope actually waved in Bobby and Sheila's direction!

L et me kill you off — it will be good for you. That was the suggestion *Brookside* Producer Mal Young made to actress Annie Miles, who played Sue Sullivan. And his powers of persuasion led to the dramatic double murder scenes of October 1991, which had millions of viewers trying to guess whodunnit.

Mal says: 'Annie had come to see me around Christmas 1990 to say that she was thinking of leaving the show. She said: "When do you think I should go?" Now we'd only just got her married to Terry but I went away and thought and suddenly it came to me — episode 1,000 in October. And I thought of all the publicity we could get. Phil Redmond and I talked about it for a few hours and that's how we came

up with the murder. Annie actually wanted to leave three months later, at Christmas 1991, but I said: "Go earlier, I'll give you a big splash to go out on." And that was actually better to launch her out into her new career.

'At our long-term planning meeting, which we hold in February or March each year, we took our 12 writers through the murder. The ace in the pack was baby Danny being killed as well because no other soap had killed a baby. I cynically wanted to get a reaction from the viewers — I wanted something big to tie in with episode 1,000.

'Every writer said: "It's a great story — but you can't possibly kill the baby." As soon as they said that, I thought, "Right, we're doing that because that's the reaction we want." They all fought me but I knew it would work.

'Only Phil and I knew who the murderer was going to be. I didn't tell the actors because the minute you tell them, they play murderer in the eyes — they start playing sinister. I wanted them to play so innocent that viewers would think it was going to be someone else. The result was I had three actors banging on my door all year asking desperately, "Did I do it?". '

The identity of Sue and Danny's killer remained a closely guarded secret. Mal explains: 'What we did on the day of shooting to confuse the crew and keep it secret was to dress Barry, Terry and Graeme Curtis all in white T-shirts, jeans and trainers, and also to use an extra of the same build. We decided that the shot of Sue being grabbed could be Barry, the shot of the legs could be Terry, the shot of the phone could be Graeme, and the shot up the stair-

Brookside *Producer Mal Young.*

A haunted Barry Grant (Paul Usher) went to confession to reveal that he killed Sue and Daniel Sullivan.

case could be the extra. All the crew were demanding: "Well, who was it killed her?" Even the Director didn't know which one we were going to use for transmission.'

Two babies, dressed identically, were used in the build-up but when Annie Miles fell, she was actually clutching a doll. While acknowledging the programme's constant quest for realism, it would have been a shade excessive to have had Annie plunging down on to concrete. So a low section of scaffolding was erected and Annie and the doll jumped on to a nice, soft mattress.

Mal remembers: 'The immediate reaction we got to the murder scene was, "It's OK killing the girl but killing the baby was dreadful." Everyone has become so sanitised to murder on TV!'

Mal knew that the storyline would prompt a huge mailbag but even he was astounded by the lengths to which hundreds of viewers went to try and ascertain the identity of the killer. 'I had piles of letters from people who had video'd the murder scenes and had freeze-framed the pictures. I had 80 letters alone from viewers who had counted the stitching on Barry's jeans, then found a shot of Terry and counted the stitches on his jeans. And they wrote to me saying that it couldn't have been Barry on the scaffold, it must have been Terry because the stitching was different. Other people counted the number of belt loops on the jeans, compared hairs on arms, the types of denim, or analysed the

The crew prepare for filming at the shopping parade.

tracks of the trainers as the shoe was raised in one shot. And having freeze-framed it, a lot of people magnified it, had a print taken off and sent me all the evidence! So when Barry went into confessional and said, "I did it," all these people wrote to me and said, "Oh no he didn't." It was great.

'I had always stuck with the fact that Barry would be the murderer but I was concerned about how you retain sympathy for a murderer. People said he must be caught and put away, justice must be seen to be done. But it's a fact of life that murderers are walking around free. We always aim to be realistic so I thought, "Let's go for it."

'But I admit I did get nervous in case people hated Barry so much that they'd switch off whenever he appeared. Should we say it was an accident, should we give him a cop-out? Paul Usher, who plays Barry, was nervous too. He was worried that he might get beaten up in the street. He said to me: "Are you sure you want to do this?"

'But it's worked out OK. Sure, the letters came in saying, "We hate him, he's a bastard. What more can he do to his best friend? We want to see him get his come-uppance." But the last line was always: "Please don't write him out, though." That

Ron Dixon met his match in the evil Darren Murphy (Matthew Crompton).

says it all about Barry — he's an enigma, a JR character.'

Mal was chosen by Phil Redmond two years ago to lead *Brookside* into the nineties. He has been with *Brookside* since 1984, starting out as Props Assistant before working his way up through Assistant Floor Manager, Floor Manager, Production Manager, Associate Producer and finally Producer.

The starting point for future *Brookside* storylines is the annual long-term planning meeting. 'Obviously Phil and I chat informally about ideas on a regular basis,' says Mal, 'but that two-day meeting is when the two of us meet the writ-

ing team to decide where we want to see the show going. We discuss what we want *Brookside* to do. Union issues were fine for 1982 but now we're more concerned with the individual so we thought we'd have more self-employed people in the show — hence the shops. We look around the families and decide where we're taking them over the next 12 months. Last year, we decided we wanted more stories about the kids — about peer pressure on them, pressure on them to have under-age sex, and general problems at school.' This resulted in such storylines as Owen Daniels being pestered by young Leanne Powell and Darren Murphy's gang orchestrating break-ins at school.

Every four weeks throughout the year, Mal Young, the 12 writers, the Script Editor, the Script Assistant and the Researcher meet to discuss a month's episodes. 'Our dozen writers are all very different,' says Mal.

Sammy disapproves while Leanne Powell (Vickie Gates) makes a play for Owen.

'No two are from the same background. They represent a good mix of politics, ages, and class. And we have a 50-50 split of male-female. So they all have their own opinions and they argue. The writers' forthright exchanges at these monthly meetings often form the basis for the actual scenes.

'A perfect example was the break-up of the Rogers family. We decided to write out Chrissy because we felt the only way forward for the Rogers was for them to split up. Added to which, research told us that more and more families with kids were splitting up. Here I had a family with children that the viewers had come to know and love.

'I said to Eithne Browne, who

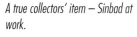

A true collectors' item – Sinbad at work.

played Chrissy: "If we don't do it this year, the whole family may have to leave next year because I think we're going round in circles with the Rogers." Chrissy was developing away from Frank. We weren't writing it — they were doing it. The character on screen was telling us what we should be doing. One of the writers said, "These two are splitting up — they've fallen out of love."

'It's sad putting actors out of work but they know it can't last forever. You can't let it get in the way of a good storyline. And when you know someone wants to leave, you can go all the way with the character. Normally, you can't go too far in case you lose sympathy for that character, but when they're leaving, it allows wider scope for us to investigate other areas.

'It was a good storyline, especially as it was seen through the eyes of a child – their daughter Katie. I wanted the feel of that kid sitting on the stairs listening to Mum and Dad arguing. But first we had to argue

ourselves into getting Chrissy to leave that family after all those years. In the end, the writers did it for me at the monthly meeting. One was taking Chrissy's point of view, while another was siding with Frank. As they were arguing across the table, I said: "Get all this down because this is the scene!" And that was what we put out.'

At these conferences, which take place four months ahead of transmission, the Researcher presents a list of things that will be happening in four months' time in Liverpool and Britain–what will be on the TV, what the big sporting events will be, as well as characters' anniversaries and birthdays.

'I suppose we play God for those two days,' says Mal, 'but I try never to go in there and say something like: "Let's do cancer and let's give it to Patricia Farnham." The storyline should come naturally out of the characters.

'I try to chat informally to the cast about ideas. Take Mickey Starke, who plays Sinbad. He was a very popular character with the audience, but where was he going? I felt he was wasted as just the comic window cleaner, I chatted with Mickey about the possibility of Sinbad having a girlfriend and perhaps discovering his past.

'Mickey gets on well with everyone in the cast and crew. We noticed his style and sense of humour were shared by Cheryl Maiker, who plays Marcia Barrett. So Sinbad and Marcia got together, even though at the time Marcia was part of Mick and Josie's story.

'We were then able to develop Sinbad and the audience began to see him in a different light–falling in and out of love, and finding his mother. His stories were a massive success with viewers, some of whom shared his tears.'

The next stage in the production cycle on *Brookside* is the commissioning meeting, where Mal brings in the four writers who are going to do that month's scripts. 'I choose the writers who I think are most suited to those scripts. Each writer has their strengths–one may be very good with the Rogers, another with the Farnhams, one's very good at humour, another at action, and so on. Each writer does a whole week's scripts – three episodes – and at that commissioning meeting I take them through the storyline and remind them of the emotions, the humour and the angst that are there.'

The writer has two weeks in which to produce a first draft, which is then delivered to Mal, the Script Editor, the Script Assistant and the Researcher. After that script has been read and discussed, the writer then has a further ten days to come up with the second draft. The artistes are scheduled and the Associate Producer decides which of the programme's six Directors is going to shoot which week's episodes. The Director then has six weeks to interpret the scripts for the

Sinbad proposes to Marcia at Goodison Park

Eat your heart out, Ringo. Keith Rooney (Kirk Smith) gives the skins a pounding.

Post - production.

Julia Brogan is mugged in the alley. What's more, the pizza's going cold.

screen. In the first week of those six, there is a writer/Director meeting, where Mal and the writer explain what they are trying to do with the story, and where they give the Director all the little hooks for future episodes.

Following a day's rehearsal for each episode, shooting takes place six weeks before transmission. The shooting week begins with a ten-hour day on the Friday and, after a weekend off, is Monday to Friday ten hours a day. It takes 60 hours to make three episodes, which works out at 11½ minutes action per day. Every Friday, there are two shoots going on – one trilogy of episodes on the last day, another on the first day. 'On a Friday, we get to the point,' says Mal, 'where there are two actors shooting in the morning – say making up after a row. Then in the afternoon, they are shooting that row from the previous week's episode. Working out of sequence can sometimes be very confusing!'

The fifth week of the cycle is rough cut week. The rough cut is just the pictures and words with neither sound effects nor music. 'It's the first time we see whether an episode has worked,' adds Mal. 'It's like getting your photos back from Boots!'

Each episode is 22½ minutes in length, and the titles and credits are added to make a total of 25 minutes. This, along with dubbing (where a door slams, a background radio or TV are added if needed), takes place during the final week of the cycle when the fine cut is done. The fine cut is essentially what goes out on screen although Mal can still add things like out-of-vision lines. 'When Julia Brogan was recovering from her mugging, Rod and Tommo were talking about her moving in, which they didn't want her to do. She went into the back room and the viewer couldn't see her but knew she was there. I got her to do a voice-over, singing "la, la, la". So suddenly she was in the scene even though nobody could actually see her. These guys were talking and you could hear "la, la, la", and you knew they didn't want her in the house. It was ten times funnier that way.

'The Saturday omnibus edition has different commercial breaks so that's put together then, too.

'On any one day, there are no fewer than 60 episodes at different

stages through the system. And of course I have to know what's going on in each one. You see, we've got six Directors all working at the same time – one is rough cutting, one is fine cutting, one is shooting, one is rehearsing, one is preparing, and one is doing recces for locations. I sometimes find myself coming out of an advanced storyline conference where we've just married someone and then I'll sit in rough cut two days later and they're arguing. I think: "Why are they arguing? They've just got married." Then I remember that in the episode I'm watching the rough cut of, they're not married yet!

'It can get confusing but it's very exhilarating. It keeps me on my toes. Other people in the television industry ask how we can retain the quality on screen with such a fast turnaround. The answer is developing the skills, talent and enthusiasm for the finished product. There's no trick, no shot cut.'

One of the most impressive features of *Brookside* is the quality of the younger actors in the cast. The majority of youngsters who join *Brookside* are plucked from ordinary schools by Casting Director Dorothy Andrew — very few have trained at stage schools. 'The talent that comes out is amazing,' enthuses Mal Young. 'I'd say we've got it right with our young actors nine times out of ten.

'We make sure we explain everything to them beforehand. Dorothy will talk to the Mums and Dads about what they're getting into, and we tell the school and the parents the worst side of it – that it could all end tomorrow. Take people like Jason Hope, who plays Rod, or Simon O'Brien, who was Damon. They came to us in their early teens, unknown and in their first job, and still at school. Suddenly they can't walk down the street anymore without being recognised. We change

The family Josie Johnson left behind.

their lives. They do all their major growing-up on screen. In effect, we're stealing their childhood.

'We only use our young actors for half a day at a time and then the chaperone takes them back to school. The exception is during school holidays, when we tend to film their major storylines. The nice thing is that the cast playing their Mums and Dads become like real parents. When Irene Marot, who plays DD Dixon, arrived, she wasn't married and had no kids. But we made her DD, wife and mother. Now she cares for the Dixon children like they're her own. You see them swapping Christmas presents – it's great.

'I remember Kevin Carson, who played Geoff Rogers, coming to see me last year. He said: "Can you kill me off? I don't want the character of Geoff to keep going. I want to be Kevin, I want to fill in the gaps and

Father Derek O'Farrell (Clive Moore) feels the strain of his relationship with nanny Margaret.

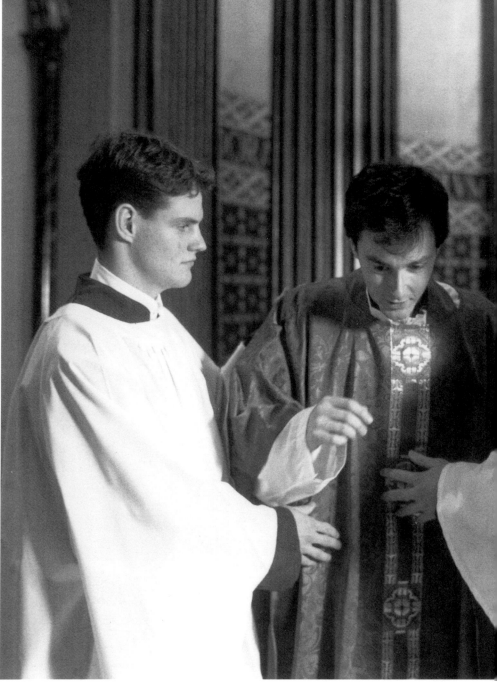

go out with my mates. I've loved it, it's been a great buzz, but I don't want to be an actor. I think it's time I left."

'I said: "Well, what with Sue and Danny, we've got too many deaths this year." Anyway, I didn't want to be negative. I wanted to do something to give young kids who aren't good at academic work some hope. Geoff had already suffered one knockback in his footballing career and he needed some cause for optimism. So when we wrote him out, we had him taken on by a football club – Torquay United. But for Kevin to come and see me and say that he

wanted out took a lot of guts.

'I never talk an actor into staying because if they're not happy, it shows on screen. You usually get to hear about impending departures through the grapevine but one who did take me by surprise was Suzanne Packer, who played Josie. Everything was fine with Josie and Mick so I had to convince myself that the character would suddenly leave. She had been wayward in the past and then some viewers said to me: "I think she's going to leave Mick." And that's what settled it for me.

'I wrote Josie out quickly because I didn't want two women – her and

doctors, patients or taxi drivers. 'We like to give the artiste concerned as much information about the subject as we can,' says Mal Young. 'But other than that, we don't let them see the storylines in advance because, in reality, you don't know what's going to happen in your life. They should be surprised.

'Basically, if we can make people think at the end of an episode for just five minutes about an issue we've raised–say, cancer–then we feel we've done our job.

Occasionally we've done a bit to much preaching in the past but I don't want to get on my soap-box. We're here to provide entertainment, but hopefully of the thought-provoking variety.

'The other important thing to remember is that, although some of us get our names credited at the end of the show each week, there are around 120 people who all make a valuable contribution to getting the show on air.'

Sue– leaving in the same month of the show. Sometimes the decisions that are made for you are the best ones: we got a year's storyline out of Mick bringing up those two kids and all the sympathy there is for that guy. Statistics tell you that the plight of the single parent is upper-most in a lot of people's minds, so I thought: "Great, I'm doing it in the show, I'm reflecting what's going on." In retrospect, Suzanne did me a favour.'

Whenever a major storyline is looming, *Brookside's* researcher will ensure authenticity by interviewing the relevant parties, be they priests,

ROADSHOW

Have you ever wondered what it would be like to be on the receiving end of a tirade from Frank Rogers? Or to discuss the price of a tin of pineapple chunks with Ron Dixon? Well, the opportunity is there for those who attend *Brookside's* script to screen lectures.

'The lectures are all part of the process of us trying to come down out of our ivory towers and so destroy the myths of television,' says *Brookside* Producer Mal Young. 'We stage two or three a year and go to places like film festivals, and polytechnics and universities with good media courses. It's a bit like a roadshow–the crew, our actors, Directors and writers come along too, and donate their time.

'The sessions last about eight hours. In the morning, we do the theory, where either Phil Redmond or I will talk about the whole production cycle

on *Brookside*. Then we have a casting session where we choose someone from the audience and in the afternoon that person will take part in a scene–usually from one of that week's episodes. For added realism, props will bring on some item of furniture like the Dixons' sofa.

'There's also a question and answer session and we've found that *Brookside* fans are very committed to the show. They will take great pains to tell us when we get it wrong. And we're glad to listen to them.

'They don't ask things like, "What colour underpants does Barry Grant wear?" or "Is Terry married in real life?" They'll say, "You really let us down on a particular issue." It's lively and it's constructive criticism–they're critical but supportive. And it's very good for getting feedback on the show.'

4 CLOSE ENCOUNTERS

Happy eaters Owen Daniels (Danny McCall) and Matty Nolan (Tony Scoggo).

At first glance, the neat little estate on which *Brookside* Close is located seems just like any other modern suburban development. On approaching the hallowed tarmac, the only clue that there is something out of the ordinary round the corner is the presence of a barrier and a security hut. But turn the bend and it hits you — for parked outside one of the houses is Frank Rogers' old maroon Cortina. This is *Brookside*.

Mersey Television owns 13 houses on the Close of which six are used for filming. The Rogers live at number 5, Mick Johnson at 6 (the bungalow), the Farnhams at 7, the Dixons at 8, the Harrisons at 9, and what's left of the Corkhills at 10. Numbers 1-3 comprise the old technical block. Mersey Television also owns some

The residents of Brookside Close would have to be pretty desperate to buy a packet of frozen peas from Ron Dixon's Trading Post or to lash out on a pizza from Terry Sullivan's Pizza Parade — even with extra cheesy topping. On screen, the Close and the shops may be separated by a short alleyway, but in reality they are five miles apart!

Brookside Close is situated in the West Derby district of Liverpool but take a walk down the alley purporting to lead to the shops and you turn two corners and come to a dead end. That is because the new *Brookside* Shopping Parade is five miles away at Childwall and there too the other end of the alley is a path to and from nowhere.

nearby flats, which used to house the publicity and casting departments.

Phil Redmond says: 'As people moved in around us at *Brookside* Close, we became the TV company at the end of the garden. At first, the residents were very concerned about huge lighting towers, so we had an open day where we showed them just how small the cameras and so on were. We always tell them what we're doing and I think we've still got a good relationship with the neighbours.'

Brookside is allowed 16 night shoots a year. The reason for the restriction is that the lamps keep the birds awake and the birds, in turn, keep babies awake.

The first thing that strikes you about the houses is how small they are. Consequently, with a cast, crew and equipment to squeeze into a cramped lounge or kitchen, some of the furniture has to be moved out

and it's a common sight on filming days for sofas and armchairs to be strewn across the front gardens.

The natural starting point for any tour of the Close is the Corkhills' house, which, in the days of Doreen and Billy, was the only residence where a brick through the window qualified as a home improvement. It's a bit smarter these days, even allowing for the cable that runs under the lounge carpet and links up with the rest of the Close. There are acoustic tiles on the ceiling to improve the sound quality, while a camera point in the stair cupboard is linked to the production gallery.

Alterations have been made to the sets over the years to develop the visual look of each of the rooms. The Corkhills, for example, have had a dividing wall taken down and an arch put in. Stepping outside, it is immediately apparent that the front lawn still hasn't recovered from the occasion when Billy did his impression of Nigel Mansell across it.

Upstairs, none of the wardrobes in the houses are real — they're just rails with hangers and sliding doors. The Rogers' house is the only four-bedroomed one and also the only one without movable walls between the bedrooms. In all the other houses, the walls dividing the bedrooms are false and are put in when needed. Because of the compact nature of the houses, no nook or cranny is wasted. At the Dixons', one of the camera positions is in an airing cupboard!

Mick Johnson's garage is really the carpenters' shed, while the front garden of his bungalow is still rife with Harry Cross's gnomes, many of them lying horizontally as if fatally wounded in one of the many battles that have taken place on the Close over the past decade. Another fact to be gleaned is that Frank Rogers' record collection includes Chuck Berry, Marvin Gaye and the Bee Gees. The Round Table would surely

The epitome of Brookside Close — Frank Rogers' Cortina.

be disappointed if they dropped in for a drink at the Farnhams', for Max and Patricia's delicately superior white wine is actually burnt sugar and their full-bodied, fruity red is Ribena.

The person responsible for the look of the Close is the designer, Candida Boyes. 'When a new family comes into the Close,' she says, 'I discuss it with the Producer. I find out what social bracket they are in — what their jobs are, how old they are, their past history, why they're coming to the Close and what their income bracket is. Then I have to decide where they would shop.

'A lot of people probably think I just put wallpaper up in houses because I like it but the look of the house has to fit the characters who live there. For example, in homes like the Corkhills' or the Rogers', where only a moderate amount of money is coming in and a family is growing up, things would tend to be a bit battered. The exception was when Sheila married Billy because she wanted to get rid of Doreen's tastes. So we radically altered the Corkhills' living-room. Doreen had always been one for very noticeable strip pine planking on the fireplace wall and a famous big clock which she smashed. But when Sheila arrived, she needed to make her mark on the house. So we re-decorated and everything became much softer, more modern.'

Since the furniture regularly has to be shifted outside the houses to accommodate the crew, Candida has to be careful to choose suites and units that are not too big or not too heavy. There are other considerations too. Light fittings can become entangled with the sound boom so, for close-ups at the Corkhills' kitchen table, the kitchen light is taped up. It is then let down for long shots.

'Also,' says Candida, 'I try not to pick furniture with glass doors

Barbara Harrison (Angela Morant) comforts husband John (Geoffrey Leesley) during one of his asthma attacks with help from son Peter (Robert Beck).

because of the reflection. If there are cabinets with glass doors, the panes usually have to be removed before we can shoot. I couldn't give the Farnhams a black kitchen (it is slate grey and dark blue) because if you put too much black stuff on screen, people disappear into it. The vogue in modern kitchens is to be very shiny but again we can't use that because our lights reflect in it. The other danger is that, with so much cheap replica furniture available these days, it's hard to stop every house looking the same. The difference in quality doesn't necessarily show up on screen so, if you're not careful, the Rogers' can look the same as the Farnhams'.

'With the crew marching in and out, the wear and tear is enormous — particularly underfoot. So we either use an expensive tough carpet, or a cheap carpet that can simply be disposed of should it get damaged.

'The hardest thing for me was when the Sullivans bought the house off Jonathan. I couldn't change anything. They didn't have any money and they had a baby on the way, so I couldn't buy them any flash new objects. They were living within Jonathan's decorations, which meant that, from a design point of view, it was very hard to say anything much about the characters. The Farnhams, on the other hand, were quite easy. They're not chain store shoppers so I bought for them at places that do modern, hand-made British furniture with an individual look.'

Since the programme is set in Liverpool, Candida places great store in shopping locally. 'I always try and buy things in Liverpool. I wouldn't go to Shrewsbury, for instance, to buy anything for these houses unless it was for a family who travelled. For the Rogers and the Johnsons, I shop at local chain stores, just as they would.

'We also have to be very careful not to give products undue prominence. We don't cover up labels but we do try to be representative. So while in one house they might be eating a particular brand of breakfast cereal, in another house we'd show a different brand. And we have to make sure we don't hold a shot for too long on any bright piece of packaging, otherwise it could unwittingly end up looking like an advert and we would get our wrists slapped.'

Dave Jones once unwittingly provided entertainment in his days as a Props Assistant on *Brookside*. 'The story was that Damon Grant had a pet rat and someone killed it. So we got an animal handler to bring us in a live rat and a dead rat that had died from natural causes. We painted blood on the dead rat and it was all ready but then shooting the scene was delayed for a few days because of the weather. I was told to hold on to the dead rat. I said, "What do you do with a dead rat? It'll smell."

'Anyway, I put it in the freezer in the design department, where all sorts of bits and pieces are kept, and

The Max factor. Max Farnham (Steven Pinder) with the two women in his life —(left) current wife Patricia (Gabrielle Glaister) and (right) ex-spouse Susannah (Karen Drury).

promptly forgot about it. Three days later, they said: "We'll do that scene now with the rat." I took it out of the freezer and the rat was in a solid block of ice — its tail was like a dart. The Director was going mad.

'As chance would have it, the Corkhills had just acquired a microwave oven so I slipped into the Corkhills' house and put it on slow defrost. It softened up nicely. But as I was taking this cooked rat out of the microwave, John McArdle, who played Billy, walked in. From that day on, he never ever ate any prop food in that house!'

All of the houses have hot and cold running water and are properly heated. The fridges, cookers and washing machines are all in full working order, and the cars that are parked out the front are taxed and roadworthy.

The plants and flowers are real, too. 'We buy our indooor plants,' says Candida, 'but I've got three gardeners as part of my design staff and we use our own greenhouses to force outdoor flowers. This means that, although we shoot March scenes six weeks earlier, we can still provide a nice display of daffodils. Because doors are often left open, house plants can die but I hate using plastic ones. If I did, the plants would always look perfect, whereas in reality most people's house plants are a bit ragged round the edges.

'The Harrisons are very keen gardeners but they share a communal front lawn with the Corkhills, who are not exactly green-fingered. So when the gardeners are mowing the lawns, I have to stop them doing both lawns at the same time because two people living side by side wouldn't mow their lawns together. There have been times when there haven't been any nice gardens, especially when the Dixons moved in and there was a load of junk outside. Everyone said, "The Close looks horrible." I said, "It's

supposed to." I actually have to restrain the gardeners from making the gardens too neat. Many's the time I've had to stop them planting things at the Corkhills'.'

Amidst all this reality, there is one fake on the Close — the letterbox. But that doesn't deter visitors from posting letters in it.

In 1990, the headquarters of Mersey Television moved to Childwall where the company bought a former further education college. 'To expand to three nights a week, we needed a second base,' says Phil Redmond. 'The good thing about it is that, because it was an educational centre, it wasn't subject to building regulations or planning laws. So different blocks have different types of brick. For us, it's a Godsend — it looks like more than one location.'

It has certainly been put to good use. The old art block was used as the police station in Mersey Television's series *Waterfront Beat* and also as the gaming machine arcade during the rent boy storyline in *Brookside*. The back of the gymnasium is used as the front entrance to *Brookside* Comprehensive, while inside signs like 'Maternity', 'Intensive Care' and 'Physiotherapy' reveal that the the science wing corridor doubled as a hospital when Patricia Farnham had her operation. Another room was once occupied by Chrissy Rogers when she was school secretary. Now the same office belongs to Barbara Harrison in her capacity as Deputy Headmistress. Other rooms have been converted into technical suites, while wardrobe and make-up can be found in former changing-rooms.

But the pride and joy of Childwall is the new *Brookside* Shopping Parade which is actually a smart, modern facade built on to the front of the old science wing. Candida Boyes recalls: 'My brief was to turn this 1950s classroom block into a

A funny thing happened on the way to the theatre — Max Farnham perched on the trolley as he comforts wife Patricia.

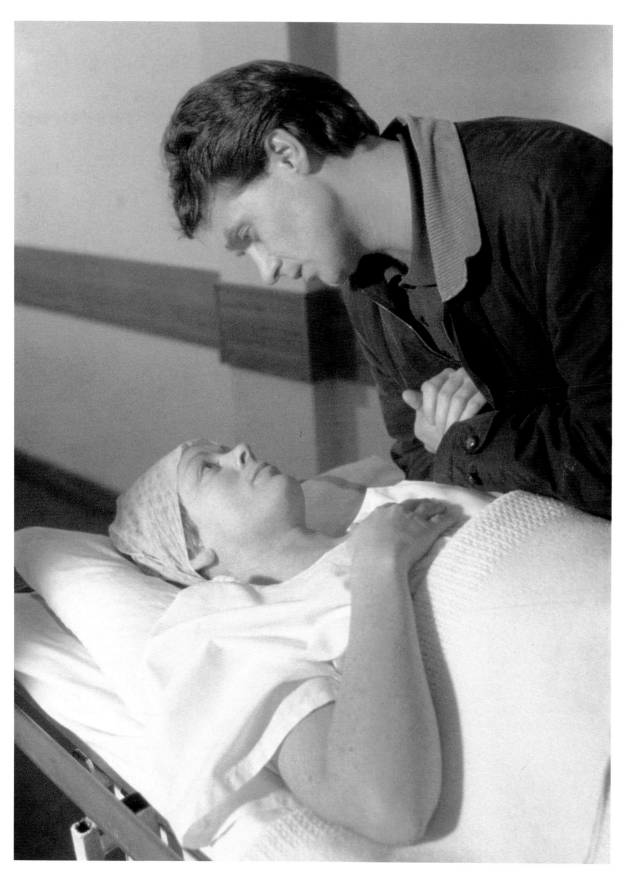

modern shopping precinct. Ron Dixon's Trading Post was half of a domestic science classroom!

'We couldn't break the concrete skeleton of the building or we would have destroyed the structure but we could break the bricks in between. Wherever there was a window became a shop unit. If it was a big space, I partitioned it into smaller units. Work started on the conversion in January 1991 and we were filming there by July.'

The food in Ron's shop looks real enough on screen but anyone shopping for a dinner party would be well advised to look out for the packets of pate filled with sand, the foam bread and the plaster sausages. 'Most of the food at the Dixons' is real,' says Candida. 'With the sausages, if someone is to be seen buying them, we swap back to genuine ones. But we try to keep perishable stuff to a minimum and the freezer is never on because it would interfere with the sound, which picks up the buzz off the motors in the freezer fan. So all the packaging in Ron's freezer is empty. Unfortunately, though, sometimes the actors put their sandwiches in the cold cabinet while filming, and then forget about them. We then go back a week later and have a horrible surprise when we open the cabinet door...

'The hairdressing salon was more complicated, as I needed to sort out all the plumbing. Also I wanted a corporate image, as the owner, Kenny Roberts, is supposed to own other salons. I wanted a look that could conceivably be reproduced in other salons because it was very distinctive. Having found a styling unit that existed, everything else in that salon was designed around it — it was all made for me. And we bought all the equipment.

'With Pizza Parade, we established that this particular pizza parlour doesn't make its own bases. It

Brookside's answer to Masterchef. Matty Nolan (Tony Scoggins) offers the condiments of the chef while Owen Daniels (Danny McCall) punishes a pizza.

buys them in and puts on its own toppings. So we get a stack of bases from a pizza product wholesaler. And when Owen was making pizzas before your eyes, we had to have plenty of bases ready. In the event of re-takes, poor old Owen could have ended up piling tomato puree

WHO LIVES WHERE

1982-9	The Grants		
1989-	The Rogers	Number	**5**

1982-4	Alan Partridge		
1984-90	Harry Cross (with wife Edna, 1984-5), (with Ralph Hardwick 1985-9)		
1990-	The Johnsons	Number	**6**

1983	Harry and Edna Cross		
1984-7	Sandra Maghie, Pat Hancock and (until 1985) Kate Moses Later, Terry Sullivan and lodgers Mick, Mike, Gill Beaconsfield		
1987-9	The Rogers'		
1989-90	The Chois		
Early 1990	Sinbad - caretaker for the Chois		
1990-	The Farnhams	Number	**7**

1982-90	The Collinses		
1990-	The Dixons	Number	**8**

1982	Heather and Roger Huntington		
1983-6	Heather (under her maiden name of Haversham)		
1986	Heather and Nicholas Black		
1987	Jonathan Gordon-Davies and Laura Wright		
1987-90	Jonathan Gordon-Davies (with first Terry Sullivan as lodger, then Terry and Sue as tenants)		
1991	The Sullivans		
1991-	The Harrisons	Number	**9**

1982-3	The Taylors		
1984-5	The Jacksons		
1985-	The Corkhills	Number	**10**

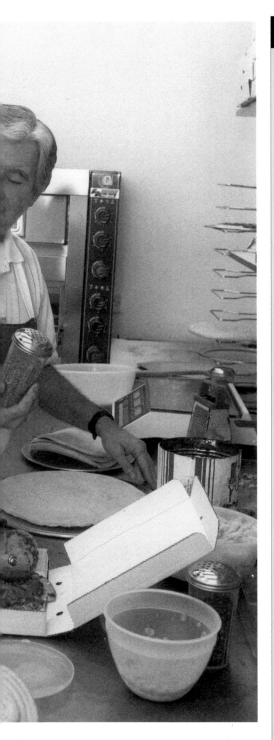

on a dozen or so bases.'

There is, however, one slight draw-back with acting in real houses. Actors are prone to forget that they are not at home and sometimes they forget to switch off their radio microphones when they go to the lavatory...

Brookside is a revolutionary soap. Not only has it pioneered shooting techniques and forced its rivals to get out on location, but it has also consistently tackled controversial issues. Until *Brookside* came along, an issue in soap terms would be Jill Richardson pondering how best to decorate the Crossroads Motel Christmas tree or *Emmerdale Farm*'s Matt Skilbeck deeply contemplating whether it was too muddy to get the tractor out.

But *Brookside* changed all that. Unemployment, drug abuse and rape were all tackled in the early years. Some other soaps realised they had to follow. Within two years of Sheila Grant being raped in July 1986, Kathy Beale met a similar fate in *EastEnders*.

Inevitably, hard-hitting storylines and realistic language didn't meet with everyone's approval. In those first weeks, the moralistic *Sun* counted the number of swear words per week in *Brookside*, Liverpool's *Daily Post* predicted that the programme would be scrapped and, of course, there were the statutory complaints from Mary Whitehouse and the National Viewers' and Listeners' Association.

Gradually, *Brookside* and the press settled down and, by 1984, the *Sunday People* was describing the show as 'the Rolls-Royce' of soaps. Even *The Times* admitted that *Brookside* had class.

Phil Redmond, still seen by some as the enfant terrible of British television, likens his role as Executive Producer to that of a Features Editor on a national newspaper. 'You can't do the topicality as such but you can plug into the trends and themes that are running through society. One of the biggest reactions

> 'I watched the very first episode of *Brookside* and was immediately enthralled with its mixture of gritty realism, Merseyside humour and willingness to deal with social controversy. Sometimes it seems as if the most infuriating characters — like Harry Cross, Barry Grant and Sinbad — were also the most attractive, but I, with a lot of viewers, really conceived a deep affection for all the characters who lived in or visited the Close. Indeed one of the most appealing aspects of *Brookside* is the fact that it is a slice of life and that we in the audience are living through the joys, sorrows and sometimes absurdities that make up REAL life.'
>
> *Through the Keyhole* guide **Loyd Grossman**

we had recently was to DD Dixon not being prepared to buy her daughter Jackie expensive training shoes to wear for school. That touched on the reality of life. We actually got more reaction to that than to Sue's murder, or to the Derek and Margaret storyline.

'We like to think we're on the ball. We did chatlines shortly after they were introduced because, to us, it was an obvious problem. We had Tracy Corkhill running up a huge phone bill at home. But it has taken people four years to wake up to the situation — it's only recently that they've started kicking up a fuss.'

The recent breast cancer storyline

involving Patricia Farnham also resulted in a large mailbag. Producer Mal Young says: 'The cancer organisations thanked us for highlighting it and a lot of individuals wrote to me to say how glad they were that we'd drawn people's attention to it.

'On the other hand, some people thought we should have shown their version of the story. They said, "You got it wrong — I didn't react like that." So we had this amazing split. I had to write back saying, "Sorry, but I can't feature thousands of people's individual stories." I have to take a bit of everyone's and then it has to fit the character. Not everyone who went through breast cancer was also going through the insecurity of worrying about her husband and his ex-wife, as Patricia was. She had a particular set of problems, and a particular set of reactions.'

Having increased public awareness on the subject, *Brookside* didn't just leave it at that. Channel Four funded a special helpline for breast cancer sufferers, manned by advisors and doctors.

A particularly courageous storyline was that which saw young priest Derek O'Farrell fall for the Farnhams' nanny Margaret. Religious topics are often taboo on television but, far from outraging Catholics, the few complaints that *Brookside* received on the subject were from Protestants who were worried that Catholics might be upset.

Mal Young remembers: 'A lot of people wrote to me anonymously saying: "This is happening in my parish, I'm glad you're highlighting it. We're told it doesn't happen. We know it does but it's just brushed under the carpet."

'My background's Catholic so I obviously had a personal interest in the story. People from my own parish were not slow to give me their criticisms of the story. We wanted to do the story sensitively — we didn't want Derek just dropping his trousers. I didn't want to shock just for the sake of it.

'A lot of people could have been hurt by it but in fact the Catholic press were very complimentary about the way we portrayed the priest. And Clive Moore, who plays Derek, is so responsible to his character.

'The illiteracy storyline threw up a lot of feedback from viewers. Some felt we'd got it wrong. How could Diana possibly be illiterate and hold down a good job? But that was the whole point. She had a career (she worked in a pharmacy) and she got through life. Illiterate people are very clever at covering it up.

Forbidden love – Derek and Margaret.

Phil Redmond.

'We got a good reaction from adult education groups, who were pleased that at last someone was taking illiteracy seriously. We also got a lot of letters from people who worked in pharmacies saying, "How dare you show that anyone who can't read or write can work in a pharmacy!" Yet we had been very careful to show that she worked on the make-up counter, not prescriptions.' In addition, *Brookside* became involved in Adult Learners' Week, which took place in March.

Another successfully tackled issue was dyslexia, as portrayed by schoolboy Geoff Rogers. At the request of the British Dyslexia Association, *Brookside* and Walker Books produced a paperback based on the storyline and entitled *Geoff's Story*, which raised funds for the BDA. The entire Rogers family went to a reception at the House of Commons to launch BDA Awareness Week.

Further praise came from the British Meningitis Trust, who were impressed with the thoroughness of the research into the story where little Daniel Sullivan contracted the illness.

By its very nature, *Brookside* is bound to run into the odd spot of bother with the broadcasting authorities. 'But I think viewers are more robust than TV executives give them credit for,' says Phil Redmond. 'We did a scene once with Tracy Corkhill and her boyfriend Jamie where her Dad Billy found a packet of Durex. We had a complaint from the IBA (as it was then) saying the shot of the Durex was on far too long, something stupid like 1.83 seconds. Channel Four asked me for a response. So I thought about it and wrote back to explain that we were very concerned about AIDS (it was at the time of the first wave of concern about AIDS) and that we held on to the shot of the packet of Durex for longer than some people might think necessary for two reasons. One was to make sure that the message was getting across that, if Tracy and Jamie were up to any-

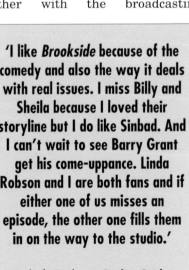

'I like *Brookside* because of the comedy and also the way it deals with real issues. I miss Billy and Sheila because I loved their storyline but I do like Sinbad. And I can't wait to see Barry Grant get his come-uppance. Linda Robson and I are both fans and if either one of us misses an episode, the other one fills them in on the way to the studio.'

Birds of a Feather star **Pauline Quirke**

thing, they were practising safe sex. Secondly, all the research shows that the people who most need the information are the ill-educated and the illiterate, and research also shows that people who are illiterate get through life by recognising the design of things. As Durex is also a generic term for contraceptives, we immediately put on screen a graphic image that even people who couldn't read would be able to recognise.

'In truth, the shot was probably only that length to make the overall edit work, but the IBA responded with a typical, "absolutely marvellous." It's strange. They kick off because they think we're just putting it in for the sake of it. Even if it is a lousy edit, so what? But you give them this long, considered — and perhaps bullshit — answer and

> '**I'm a big fan of *Brookside* and if ever I miss an episode, I make sure I watch the Saturday omnibus. What I like about *Brookside* is that it shows life as it really is. It's so believable and extremely well written and well acted. And although it's not afraid to tackle issues head on, it's never patronising. Above all, it's great entertainment. My favourite characters at the moment are Sinbad, Margaret and the Farnhams but I was very fond of Sheila and Billy. I didn't think the relationship between them would ever work but they were superb. I particularly remember their first kiss after all that pussy-footing around. It was a magic moment.'**
>
> Television presenter **Lorraine Kelly**

they say, "Fine. Thanks." And it's in the file. I do think regulators worry too much about what might happen instead of waiting to see what really does.

'It was much the same when I thought about killing a dog on screen. Part of my role is to decide when the show needs pepping up a bit — it's a gut feeling. One time I went to the storyline conference and I said, "We need something to get people talking about the show." At the time, Barry was involved with Sizzler, the gangster, and I was getting concerned that Sizzler was becoming a hero because the public always love the bad guys. It wasn't right because Sizzler was the force of evil and Barry the force of good. So I told the writers, "I want an act that shows that, no matter how funny or entertaining Sizzler is, this is a guy who hurts people. He's evil.

And what he should do is kill a dog, chop its head off."

'In Britain, killing animals is worse than shooting people. The writers immediately said, "You can't kill a dog on screen."

'I said, "Why not?"

'They said, "You just can't."

'Anyway, I forced it through the storyline conference. The story was that Sizzler was trying to get hold of a gaming arcade and Barry was supposed to be the muscle man. The woman who owned the arcade was Ma Johnston and it was her dog.

'None of the writers wanted to do this. They said, "It's terrible. Can't we just frighten the dog?"

'I said, "No, chop the dog's head off. It's the *Godfather* scene with the horse's head — it's what we need. Sizzler's got *The Godfather* out on video and thinks it's marvellous so he tells Barry to kidnap the dog and chop its head off if Ma Johnston doesn't hand over the arcade."

'The writer who had to do it, Barry Woodward, said: "I can't chop a dog's head off." But the first draft came in and, to give him his due,

'The day they were due to shoot the scene, I got a phone call from location. "We've just got to the scene with the dog. Is it absolutely essential?"

'I said, "Shoot the scene — I'll look at it in editing." I went into editing, saw the rough cut but they hadn't edited it right. They'd moved the scene. I said, "Where's the scene?"

'So they re-edited it and there was another protest. I said, "Just get it edited."

'The tape was delivered to Channel Four and I got another phone call. "We don't know about this dog's head scene." But I talked them round and it went out on air. The whole world went up. Our switchboards and the Channel Four switchboard lit up with calls protesting, "How dare you threaten a dog's life!"

The Rogers' and Geoff's mate Bumper (second right) urge safety on November 5. Unfortunately, Frank and Chrissy's marriage soon lost its sparkle and fizzled out like a damp squib.

he'd researched it — he'd found out how you chop a dog's head off and he'd got plastic sheets to put around it and so on. The script went out but as they were typing it in admin., I got the feedback that they weren't happy. I said, "It's got nothing to do with you."

'It went into rehearsals and the Director said, "We can't do this."

'I said, "Just do it."

'Then word came back that the cast weren't happy about the dog's head being chopped off. I said, "Go and shoot the scene."

'When I was pregnant six years ago, it became a ritual for me to sit down with a giant cup of tea and crumpets with raspberry jam to watch the Saturday omnibus edition of *Brookside*. And it's still a ritual to this day. My whole Saturday centres around it. For that hour and a half, no one dares to interrupt me — it's often my only chance of peace in the whole week. What I like about *Brookside* is that it's honest and as truthful as it's possible to be in a TV drama. It's certainly the most realistic of all the soaps. I used to enjoy Damon Grant — he was a good scally — but my present favourite is definitely Ron Dixon. He's absolutely wonderful.'

The Help Squad presenter **Annabel Giles**

> **'Brookside** appeals to me because it has the right balance in all respects — in its storylines, its characters, its locations and in its light and shade between the serious issues and comic situations.'
>
> *Going Live* presenter **Sarah Greene**

'The scene was at the end of the episode. Barry looked at the dog and said, "It's either you or me," because earlier in the episode Sizzler had told him: "If you don't chop the dog's head off, I'll chop your head off." So Barry took the knife and we went out on the music. That's all it was. That was on the Wednesday and the Saturday omnibus and what happened the following Monday was that Barry hadn't had the heart to kill the dog. But nobody would wait and we had 200 complaints.

'When Sheila Grant was raped, we only had 60 complaints. With the rape scene, on the Wednesday we transmitted it with the guy throwing his coat over her head and dragging her into the bushes. Following complaints, Channel Four said they were editing the scene out for the omnibus edition. So on Saturday, she turned and they cut to a shaking bush and then up came the credits. I thought that was far worse. Sure enough, on the Wednesday, they'd had something like 20 complaints but on the Saturday they had 60, mostly after Channel Four's decision to cut the scene.'

But the biggest drama in the first ten years of *Brookside* occurred early in 1992. As a result, the merest mention of episode 1049 is guaranteed to turn grown Producers into quivering wrecks. It followed Fran Pearson revealing to Terry that Barry had had sex with Sue.

Mal Young reflects: 'After that, we knew that the audience would be waiting on the edges of their seats to see what Terry would do. I decided that Terry should throw a chip pan full of hot fat over Barry and we'd cut there on the Friday night. Then on the Monday, we pan around the empty room, we don't know what's happened, we see the empty chip pan on the floor and the wreckage from the fight, then we see Barry coming into the room with all his arm burned and his jacket ripped to form a makeshift bandage. And as Barry comes in, Terry jumps out from behind him, holds a knife to his throat and the fight continues, picking up from Friday.

'The writers thought it sounded great and went ahead and did it. But Friday's episode was directed by a different Director and crew from Monday's and they hadn't talked to each other. I watched the Friday episode in rough cut and it was terrific. The following week I saw the rough cut of the Monday episode. We pan around the room, Barry comes in but he hasn't been touched. He's got his suit on and with just a little bandage across his fingers.

'I said, "What's happened to the chip pan?"

' "Ah," they said. "We've discussed this — the chip pan missed him."

'I said, "You've missed the point — we'll have to re-shoot it."

'But that was easier said than done. Paul Usher had gone on holiday, couldn't be contacted and wouldn't be back before transmission. So we got Brian Regan, who plays Terry, back in and re-shot one side of the fight. We'd got all the shots of Barry so this time I got Terry to throw the chip pan on the floor in anger, look up, pick up a knife, then come towards him. That will explain how Barry gets cut.

'That was OK. But then the ITC heard that *Brookside* had a knife scene and asked to see the episode. They decreed that the knife could stay in the Friday episode after 8pm

The s-s-s-sinister Sizzler.

but had to be cut from the Saturday omnibus. Then they saw Monday's episode, where Terry holds the knife to Barry's throat. They said, "That cannot go out at any time of day."

'This all happened on the Friday before the Monday transmission. On the Saturday, Paul Usher came back from his holiday abroad with a full suntan. We waited outside his house for him to arrive and brought him straight in. The script was re-written on the Saturday morning and, in the afternoon, we put a crew together to shoot the new scene. This time, Barry comes in with no bandage, looks around and Terry is still there. But we had to analyse why Barry had the bandage for the rest of the episode otherwise we'd have had to shoot the whole episode that afternoon. So we had Barry grabbing the door to go out and Terry trapping Barry's hand in the door.

'We stood there waiting for

Securicor at 8.00 that night with the scene that we'd just cut. We had to rush it through because it had to be at Channel Four by 10am the next day to be copied and sent to S4C, as Wales take it earlier on Mondays. That was certainly the closest I've ever got...'

> 'My favourite *Brookside* character is Sinbad — he's one of the great tragi-comic creations of all time. The things I like about *Brookside* are its realism and its humour. Had it been set in Barnsley, it would have been perfect. But I do miss Heather — I used to fancy her like mad. It's about time they brought her back.'
>
> Media personality **Michael Parkinson**

6
WHO'S WHO
BARRY GRANT

Paul Usher as Barry Grant.

'm glad we're seeing the nasty side of Barry Grant,' says Paul Usher. 'I wanted to make him more evil. He's a more interesting character than just a Mammy's boy.'

Barry was always the apple of Sheila Grant's eye but he has turned out to be rotten to the core. In the early days, he was more of a Jack the lad, forever concocting money-making schemes with his mate Terry. He fancied himself as a bit of a hard case and was only too willing to sort out family problems, usually with his fist. But then he began to get involved with bosses of the Liverpool underworld like Tommy McArdle, and his eye for the ladies nearly landed him in big trouble when he chased after the girl-friend of stuttering gangster Sizzler. Barry was lucky not to be s-s-silenced for good.

Epitomising the self-made man spirit of the late eighties, he moved into the seedy world of acid house parties before acquiring the *Brookside* Parade of five shops. Barry has become a major property owner – a man of power. And power corrupts. Besides, there was always the suspicion that Barry was capable of real violence — remember how he put the wind up hardman Joey Godden with a shotgun. The murder of Sue and Daniel and the subsequent threats to Fran Pearson merely emphasised that Barry Grant is a pretty unpleasant piece of work.

Barry has only ever been interested in one person in his life — himself. He never forgave his doting mother for moving in with and marrying Billy Corkhill and he never got on with Bobby, the man he thought was his father. Sure, Barry came from a broken home but he helped break it. And he showed his true colours when he slept with the wife of his supposed best pal Terry and then killed her. With friends like Barry, who needs enemies? He's had a few moments of genuine grief — when Tracy Corkhill aborted his baby and when he found out that Matty Nolan was his real father — but most people would like to see him suffer a lot more yet.

Producer Mal Young says: 'Paul was very interested in the change of direction for Barry, to become a shady businessman. For a start, he got a suit out of it! That appealed to him, to get out of his jeans for a few

episodes. And we've done it without losing the heart of Barry Grant. He's still Sheila Grant's son, the lad from Liverpool.'

Paul adds: 'I would like to show a bit more of Barry's conscience because he's very lonely and I reckon he goes through hell. He certainly suffered over the death of Sue and Danny — that's why he finally had to tell Terry exactly what happened.'

Paul Usher, 32 and single, is the only survivor from the very first episode of *Brookside*. He was born in Liverpool and much of his early career was devoted to music. Before joining *Brookside*, he toured America with his band *20/20* as singer and bass guitarist. He was also a Blue Coat at Pontin's where he used to entertain the campers.

Every year, Paul spends up to three months away from *Brookside*

while Barry is off on some dodgy business deal. 'It's partly to recharge my batteries. It's hard work playing Barry and without taking a break each year, I wouldn't have been able to carry on for as long as I have. Also, it gives me a chance to get back in touch with the real world. In the past, I've gone and lived in a caravan and got a job at a garden centre digging ditches, laying turf and shifting sand. I've also helped out on a farm. It helps keep my feet on the ground and makes sure that when I come back to *Brookside*, I'm raring to go.'

Has he noticed a change in the public's perception of Barry over the years? 'The public used to come over and chat to me but now I think they're frightened of Barry so they tend to back off. I don't get any fan mail anymore either!'

Paul Usher as Barry Grant.

WHO'S WHO
TRACY CORKHILL

'I wouldn't want to meet Tracy Corkhill,' says Justine Kerrigan, 'and I certainly wouldn't want to have my hair done by her.

Quite. You always got the feeling with Tracy that she was likely to slip concentrated acid into the perming lotion if it was a customer she didn't like. Wilful, headstrong and often downright surly, Tracy was no great loss to the diplomatic corps. Justine admits: 'At first, a lot of people didn't like her. They used to think, "Little cow!" She wound people up and managed to fall out with everyone at work.

In fairness, being a Corkhill is not exactly the ideal start in life but Tracy's attitude put everybody's back up. She could be as stubborn as her father Billy. The atmosphere between the two wasn't helped by Billy finding out about his daughter's relationship with geography teacher Peter Montague. He received a three-month suspended prison sentence for attacking Montague. Then Tracy had a long-term boyfriend, the slovenly Jamie Henderson. Billy didn't rate him but Tracy got her own back when Billy became serious with Sheila Grant.

'She certainly didn't make it easy for Billy and Sheila,' says Justine, 'but then she's never been afraid to speak her mind. I think part of the problem was that she actually liked Sheila but didn't want to.'

Possibly to spite Billy and Sheila, Tracy took up with Barry Grant and, despite Barry's pleas, ended up having an abortion. 'That was a really powerful storyline,' says Justine. 'Afterwards, I did get a shock though when a girl I'd never met before came up to me in a nightclub and started telling me about her abortion. Even though I didn't want to, because it was nothing to do with me, I felt obliged to listen.'

Justine Kerrigan has played Tracy for over seven years. Her grandfather is veteran film and television actor Peter Kerrigan, best remembered for his role in *Boys From The Blackstuff*. 'It was my grandfather who encouraged me to go for *Brookside'* she says.

Unlike Tracy, 21-year-old Justine has settled down and is married to computer expert Simon Kennedy. And in 1991, Tracy was sent off on a world hairdressing cruise while Justine gave birth to daughter Hollie.

Eagle-eyed *Brookside* viewers may remember that before appearing as Tracy, Justine was briefly seen as one of Damon Grant's girlfriends.

Justine Kerrigan as Tracy Corkhill.

JULIA BROGAN

'I based a lot of Julia on my grandmother,' says actress Gladys Ambrose. 'I borrowed some of her favourite sayings like "Now get in there, Lady Godiva" and "Spare me!"

'As youngsters, we were always having parties at which my grandmother used to sing *Nellie Dean*. So when in *Brookside*, Julia had to step in at the last minute and sing at the Commonwealth and Empire Club, I took a leaf out of my grandmother's book and sang *Nellie Dean*. Funnily enough, she was never in showbusiness, though I think she would like to have been.'

Gladys's TV debut came in the play, *Match of the Day*. 'Bill Dean, who played Harry Cross in *Brookside*, was my husband in that. Then I did another play, *Bag of Yeast*, where Bill played my brother and where Peter Kerrigan played my husband. Now Peter's granddaughter Justine is my granddaughter Tracy in *Brookside*! No wonder in London they used to call us the Liverpool Repertory Company.'

Gladys, whose other roles include that of Eddie Yeats' landlady in *Coronation Street*, still does numerous charity shows and pantos. 'I perform at a lot of old people's homes and old soldiers' reunions where I specialise in songs from the shows.' Her daughters, Janette and Wendy, have their own singing act under the name of The Votel Sisters and Gladys is the proud grandmother of two-year-old Richard.

In *Brookside*, to the uninitiated, Julia (Doreen Corkhill's mother) seems an interfering busybody whose ideal form of transport would be a broomstick. But Gladys is quick to defend her. 'I love Julia,' she says warmly. 'I know she speaks before she thinks but she's the salt of the earth and she'll always turn up trumps when someone's in trouble. She's the sort who would bring them into the world and lay them out when they're dead.'

Julia has been unlucky in love. She was turned down by Harry Cross and then, just when it looked as if she had nailed Cyril Dixon, he was inconsiderate enough to die. 'She was devastated about Cyril,' laments Gladys, 'but she'll always pick herself up, dust herself down and start all over again. She's a great survivor.

'I get fan mail from all ages — I've had Mums in the street get their little ones to show me their impressions of Julia. And I got plenty of reaction when Ron Dixon accused her of stealing. At that time, whenever I went into a shop, people would say: "Watch the till, here's Julia..."'

Gladys Ambrose as Julia Brogan.

WHO'S WHO
ROD CORKHILL

The Force is no longer with him — Jason Hope as Rod Corkhill.

'Unlike his Dad and his uncle, Rod has stuck to the straight and narrow,' says 22-year-old Jason Hope. 'He's got a strong social conscience, which is why — even though he loves Diana — he put the problems of Craig the rent boy before his own wedding day.' While Diana was waiting at the church, Rod was lying in a public lavatory at Lime Street Station after being beaten up by Craig's pimp.

Rod's time in the Merseyside Force has had its ups and downs. He and his best friend Tommo (P.C. Neil Thompson) helped bust a dog-fighting ring but during Operation Hickory, he witnessed Tommo being stabbed and was investigated by senior officers. Then after disobey-

Most fathers would be horrified to learn that their son had got a job as chauffeur to an international drug smuggler or as ticket collector in a brothel. But to Billy Corkhill and his brother Jimmy, son Rod had brought the ultimate shame on the family name — he'd become a policeman.

Rod is the white sheep of the Corkhills — the only male member of the clan to operate on the right side of the law. It took a lot of getting used to. After all, a Corkhill as a copper is like one of the Krays becoming a social worker.

ing orders with regard to the Craig case, he was suspended from duty. Lastly, he was slashed across the face during the hair salon raid — the wounding which finally made him quit the force, at Diana's insistence. Rod was engaged to the prim nurse Kirsty Brown but he wanted a bit of excitement in his life and asked W.P.C. Emma Reid to accompany him to her bedroom. When Kirsty spotted them together on his 21st birthday trip to Blackpool, the engagement was off.

Although he may not have thought so at the time, splitting up from Kirsty was a lucky escape for Rod. She was old before her time and looked as if she had the potential to nag execessively. She could well have been born to wield a rolling pin. Anyway, Rod wasn't ready to settle down then – at least, not with Kirsty. 'After falling out with Kirsty, he was disappointed

when Emma didn't want a more permanent relationship,' adds Jason. 'So now he just wants the steady lifestyle, which is what he thinks he's got with Diana. But he's got a nasty shock in store.'

Jason made his acting debut at the age of ten as Fagin in a school production of *Oliver Twist*. 'That started me off and I then worked at the Liverpool Everyman and the Neptune Youth Theatres while I was still at school. I also did bits of television, including an episode of Alan Plater's *The Beiderbecke Affair* in which I was seen mowing a lawn.'

Jason didn't let the grass grow under his feet and in 1985, when he was 15 and in his final year at school, he joined *Brookside*. 'I was at the Everyman at the time and the casting people from *Brookside* came to take a look at some of us. I got the call and then had to be matched up with Justine Kerrigan, who plays Tracy, to see whether we looked like brother and sister. Then I had to meet John McArdle (Billy) and Kate Fitzgerald (Doreen) to make sure we could pass off as members of the same family.'

Certain members of the public don't always take kindly to actors who play policemen on television. Has Jason encountered any hostility? 'Nothing heavy, just the odd comment from people who clearly don't like the police. I simply told them that I wasn't a policeman, it was just a part I played. I usually ended up chatting to them and they realised it was OK. But it reminds you that television is such a powerful medium.'

Jason, who is single and still lives in Liverpool, is a sporting fanatic. He loves tennis, keeping fit and soccer and his latest ambition is to master golf.

But he confesses that he's never nurtured the slightest ambition to be a policeman. 'I wouldn't want to be tied to one job. That's what I love about acting — the variety.'

Tracy Corkhill (Justine Kerrigan) goes through her panda phase.

WHO'S WHO
DIANA CORKHILL

Paula Frances as Diana Corkhill.

Moving house recently brought home to actress Paula Frances the painful problems experienced by her illiterate screen character, Diana Corkhill.

'It's all the forms you have to fill in,' says Paula. 'Things like the mortgage application form, even the assembly instructions for bedroom furniture — how does anyone who's illiterate cope with all that?'

Notwithstanding the fact that someone with a degree in English Language would be hard pushed to understand the instructions for self-assembly furniture, one takes Paula's point. She has researched the subject thoroughly. 'I phoned all the adult literacy places in Liverpool and when I went to Birmingham to appear on ITV's *The Time...The Place*, I met a lot of people who couldn't read or write. I can compare illiteracy to being lost in a foreign country where you can't read the signs, you can only recognise symbols.'

Paula was dismayed to find a lack of basic reading books to help illiterate adults. 'I haven't seen any grown-up version of a-b-c books. Diana had to make do with *Sammy the Squirrel*, something that must put a lot of people off, particularly teenagers.

'I received a lot of letters about Diana's illiteracy and the reaction was very positive. It made people feel that they're not on their own, even at 20. I was pleased with the story, too, because it explained why Diana always seemed a bit slow. But now that her confidence has grown, she's becoming more independent of Rod, particularly since they got married. Unfortunately she's chosen the wrong sort of friend in Peter Harrison.'

Diana is a kindly soul. There aren't too many girls who would have been prepared to give Rod a second chance following the fiasco of her wedding day. After all, it's not every bride's dream to visit the groom in casualty. But happily, she later defied her father and moved back in with Rod. She may never set the world alight with her contribution to nuclear physics but her courage and determination is overcoming illiteracy serve as an example to others.

As a child, Liverpudlian Paula was a great fan of old Hollywood

movies. 'I used to sit watching the telly when I was about five, in awe of stars like Bette Davis, Cary Grant and Marilyn Monroe. It was then that I decided I wanted to act. As an only child, I used to sing and dance a lot at home and I was quite an extrovert at school. At nine, I played Jim Hawkins in the Kirkdale County Primary School production of *Treasure Island*. It's nice because I still go back to that school to present prizes and my little cousin Laura is a pupil there now.'

After training at the Merseyside Dance and Drama Centre, followed by a theatre arts course at the Liverpool Theatre School, Paula toured Finland and Italy for seven and a half months with the Crazy Midnight Dancers' international cabaret show. 'I did dancing and choreography and it was a wonderful experience, all that travelling and taking in different cultures. It was funny because while I was at college, I'd always said that if I couldn't get my Equity card, I'd simply go away and dance. I meant it as a joke but that's exactly how it turned out!'

Brookside marks 23-year-old Paula's television debut. And away from the Corkhills', she teaches step aerobics and callanetics five nights a week in Liverpool.

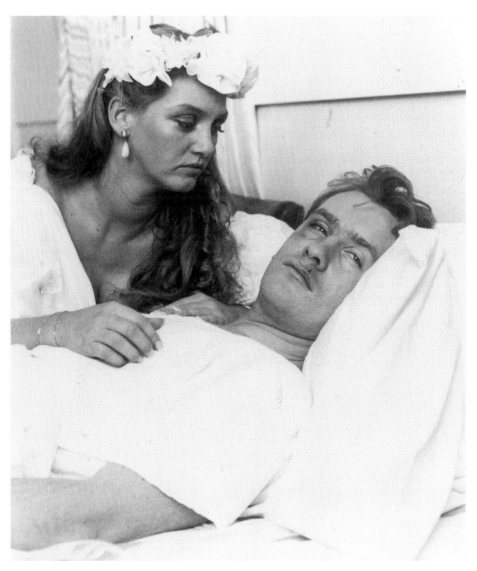

It wasn't quite the honeymoon Diana (Paula Frances) expected as she visited Rod (Jason Hope) in hospital after he had been beaten up on the day they first tried to get wed. The real ceremony went off without a hitch.

WHO'S WHO
JIMMY CORKHILL

T he sixth-formers at a Liverpool school could hardly believe their luck — their new English teacher was going to be *Brookside*'s king of knock-off, Jimmy Corkhill. Surely lessons would be like a holiday — after all, Jimmy is allergic to hard work.

But actor Dean Sullivan, who plays Jimmy and who worked as a supply teacher until 1990, had other ideas. 'I think the kids thought some scally would be teaching them but they got a rude awakening because I'm a stickler for discipline.'

Teaching was, in fact, Dean's first career. After graduating from Lancaster University with a degree

Dean Sullivan as Jimmy Corkhill.

in Drama and Education, he worked as a primary school teacher in Liverpool for six years. 'But all the time I was interested in amateur dramatics and I used to direct the school plays.

'One night I was playing Jack Worthing in *The Importance of Being Earnest* with the Neptune Theatre Group and a professional Director happened to be in the audience. I was offered the chance to get my Equity card so I decided to take the plunge. I thought, "I'll give it five years and see how it goes." But within two years, I'd got *Brookside*.

'It all started when Rob Spendlove, who had played Roger Huntington (Heather's first husband), suggested I write to *Brookside* because they're always interested in Liverpool actors. I auditioned to play one of the brothers of Vicky Cleary who were involved in a van warfare with Terry Sullivan and Pat Hancock. I didn't get the part but they knew Jimmy was coming up and were saving me for that.

'Jimmy was originally down for just six episodes as a foil to Billy during the storyline between Tracy and the teacher Peter Montague. But I'm glad to say he's managed to hang around ever since.'

Jimmy has done more than anyone else to turn *Brookside* into Crookside. For ages, he was the archetypal bad penny, always turning up at the Corkhills' when he wasn't wanted — which was most of the time — and trying to sell stuff that had fallen off the back of a lorry. He had more fiddles than Nigel Kennedy. As a result, his relationship with elder brother Billy was sometimes strained. Billy was no stranger to the odd scam but he

wasn't amused when Jimmy built him a garage with stolen bricks.

Even Jimmy's chat-up lines are hot. Separated from wife Jackie, he took up with Sheila Grant's best friend Kathy Roach, if only because she worked in a bookmaker's. But recently he managed to work his way back into Jackie's affections despite the opposition of their son, Jimmy Junior, who had never forgotten catching Jimmy playing happy families in bed with Jackie's sister Val.

Dean Sullivan says: 'Jimmy's a lovable rogue who has always been just on the wrong side of the law. But he was mortified when his daughter Lindsey said she didn't want him at her wedding and he became very sad and lonely. That's when he started getting into heavier crime but he was out of his depth with Joey Godden — he hasn't got

the bottle for it. All that business made him realise that he wanted to settle down at last. So he's been trying hard to make a go of it again with Jackie.

'But old habits die hard and anyway I wouldn't want him to go completely straight. The public like him the way he is because, let's face it, everybody knows somebody like Jimmy with his cheeky grin and quick repartee.'

Since he has become a regular on *Brookside*, Dean, who is single and still lives in Liverpool, has had to pack in his supply teaching. 'There simply isn't the time anymore,' he says. But Dean does still have time to collect modern paintings and ceramics. It's hard to imagine Jimmy enjoying such an artistic hobby — unless they'd been featured on *Crimewatch UK*.

Jackie and Jimmy Corkhill pretend to be honeymooners at the Adelphi hotel in Liverpool.

WHO'S WHO
JACKIE CORKHILL

S ue Jenkins couldn't believe her luck when her husband walked into Ron Dixon's shop. No, not screen spouse Jimmy Corkhill but her real-life husband, actor David Fleeshman, familiar to fans of *Emmerdale* as corrupt councillor Charlie Aindow.

Sue recalls: 'David made a guest appearance in *Brookside* earlier this year as David Hurst, who was owed money by the Harrisons. And it so happened that we were in a scene together — he walked into Ron's shop, where I was serving, to ask where the Harrisons lived. He also bought a packet of mints. It was bizarre. Of all the people he could have worked with in this one

Sue Jenkins as Jackie Corkhill.

episode of *Brookside*, it was me. And although we've done a lot of stage work together, that was the first time we had appeared together on television.

'Not that our children, five-year-old Emily and three-year-old Richard, were impressed by seeing Mummy and Daddy on the TV. When we came on, they announced that they wanted to watch the other side!'

Jimmy and Jackie Corkhill met back in 1971. He noticed her in a pub wearing tight white jeans and bought her *Never Ending Song of Love* by the New Seekers on their second date. They subsequently separated but, against all the odds, Jimmy won her back. Will they live happily ever after? Sue Jenkins doubts it.

'I don't think they'll ever be truly happy,' she says. 'The relationship

will always be turbulent. One minute she'll be throwing a plate at him, the next they'll be making up. They've both got terrible tempers but they actually enjoy the rows. And there's still a lot bubbling away underneath between them. They share the same sense of humour — there's still that vital spark.

'What worried her most about taking him back was that it split the family. Her son Jimmy Jnr. has gone and that was devastating for her. But she made a conscious decision that she didn't want to carry on hanging around singles bars so she decided to make another go of it with Jimmy. Anyway, she knew that one day her son would leave home and then she'd be alone. And she didn't want that. But she's under no illusions. She knows Jimmy so well and doesn't really expect him to change.'

Liverpool-born Sue wanted to act from the age of five but didn't make her TV debut until she was 17, when she played a naughty schoolgirl in *Z Cars*. She worked as Assistant Stage Manager at Chesterfield Civic Theatre and met her husband while she was playing Pinocchio on tour.

Apart from the Granada series *Coasting*, Sue's best-known role prior to *Brookside* was, of course, as barmaid Gloria Todd in *Coronation Street*. 'It's over three years since I left the *Street* — I was four months pregnant with Richard when I went. I suppose it's quite a coup going from one soap to another but it's nice because they are such totally different characters. Jackie will flirt with anybody whereas Gloria was more the girl-next-door type, despite the efforts of Fred Gee and Jack Duckworth. I think that, in terms of my career, Jackie has exorcised the ghost of Gloria and it's also stopped people asking me: "Were you discovered in a bar? " Such is the pulling power of the Rover's Return! '

Jackie Corkhill (Sue Jenkins) serves real - life husband David Fleeshman with a packet of mints.

WHO'S WHO
SINBAD

It's strange but true — window cleaner Sinbad, the man with the shabby shammy, is Britain's latest agony aunt. And it's all because he's found true love with Marcia Barrett.

'People suddenly see Sinbad in a different light,' says Michael Starke. 'All they ever used to call out in the street was, "Can you clean my windows?" But instead they now ask, "How's Marcia?" The public have realised how kind Sinbad is and have started to send me all these letters. They think they can write to him about their problems. It's great. I feel like Marje Proops!'

Sinbad, who is now 35, has always been a frustrated romantic (he tried an ambitious liaison with Caroline Choi) but he scaled new heights when he took Marcia, the love of his life, to Goodison Park, the home of Everton Football Club, and proposed via the electronic scoreboard. When she accepted, it was Sinbad 1 Ellis 0.

The effervescent Mickey Starke didn't turn to acting until he was 26. Before that, he had tried a variety of jobs. 'I was a commis-chef in a restaurant for a week and then I worked for a burglar alarm firm, pinning cables. But my heart wasn't in it and I was crap. I was the first apprentice they sacked. After that I got a job sweeping the roads.'

His first taste of showbusiness came when he fronted a comedy show band which toured the variety club circuit around Liverpool, Scotland and Newcastle.

'But I'd always wanted to be an actor and my chance came when I joined the Liverpool "lunch-time" theatre and was spotted by *Brookside*'s Casting Director Dorothy Andrew. In 1984 she cast me as Sinbad.'

Since then, Mickey has tackled everything from Brecht to Bleasdale and from Shakespeare's *Taming of The Shrew* to modern-day pantomime like *Wack and The Beanstalk* and *Kool, Kool, Kat*. He also starred in *No Holds Bard*, directed by former *Brookside* actress Noreen Kershaw (she played Kathy Roach), and his TV appearances include *Making Out* and *Distant Voices, Still Lives*.

Mickey, who is married with two daughters Jamie and Hayley, reflects: 'I've been lucky to be able to work in my native Liverpool for so long. I remember one of my early roles was in *Cavern of Dreams*, a play about a rock group. There I was in the full leather gear and a quiff.' Now he's happy to settle for shammy leather and a bucket.

Michael Starke as Sinbad

WHO'S WHO
MARCIA BARRETT

'Marcia and Sinbad are good for each other,' declares actress Cheryl Maiker. And she's certainly better off with Sinbad than her old flame Ellis Johnson — I wouldn't touch Ellis with a barge-pole.

Warm-hearted Marcia entered *Brookside* as an old friend of Josie Johnson's — she too had previously worked at the dubious Fourstar Club. When Josie left, it was Marcia who had to break the bad news to Mick and she often felt her loyalties divided between the two of them. But Marcia hung around and gradually her friendship with Sinbad blossomed into romance and a mutual proposal of marriage.

'Then came the rocky patch,' says Cheryl, 'when Sinbad found out that Marcia can't have children. He took it badly because he was looking forward to being a Dad. For her part, she couldn't understand why he was so upset — they'd still got one another.'

It was a harrowing storyline and one which Cheryl was able to appreciate. 'I'm lucky in that I've got a young son but a friend of mine can't have children so I know how devastating it can be.'

Cheryl, 29, was born in Liverpool although she now lives in Kent with husband Heath and two-year-old Benjamin. 'I trained at the Elliot Clarke Drama School in Liverpool where I got to know Rachael Lindsay who plays Sammy in *Brookside*.

'Like most aspiring actresses, I went through a lean spell when I had to work as a salesgirl in a High Street store. The worst part was always having to have your bags searched as you left — apparently it was standard company practice for new employees. But the woman who did the searches obviously took a dislike to me because she just used to throw all my things on the floor.

'Fortunately, I was only there for two months and then I landed the part of Hazel O'Connor's wayward daughter in the TV series *Fighting Back*. I was 21 at the time but I was playing a 15-year-old. I suppose I've always looked young for my age!

'Since then, apart from the year I took off to have Ben, I've been working non-stop. I was in *Rockliffe's Babies*, three series of the comedy *Life Without George*, in which I was Carol the receptionist, and I played the original role of Brenda in *Watching* at the Liverpool Playhouse.' Cheryl has also worked at the National Theatre for a season in *Strangeness of Others*.

Cheryl Maiker as Marcia Barrett.

WHO'S WHO
ELLIS JOHNSON

Francis Johnson as Ellis Johnson.

Oily Ellis is one of life's smoothies — and doesn't he know it! He slithers around causing trouble wherever he goes. After descending on older brother Mick without any warning, he proceeded to do his utmost to break up the relationship between his old girlfriend Marcia and Sinbad.

At first, he scored a few telling blows as Sinbad didn't know how to deal with him. But as it became apparent that Marcia preferred Sinbad, Ellis got more and more rattled and Sinbad's confidence grew.

He realised that Ellis was no longer a threat. There must have been a cheer the length of the country when Ellis directed one of his snide remarks to Sinbad up his ladder and Sinbad responded by emptying a bucket of water over Ellis's head. Ellis's humiliation was complete. He just couldn't understand why Marcia would pass over such a cool guy for a lump of lard like Sinbad.

Sinbad wasn't the only one who was less than pleased by Ellis's arrival — Mick wasn't thrilled either, particularly when he lost his cab through Ellis's irresponsibility. It was Mick who practically brought Ellis up after their father disappeared, a fact for which Ellis seems markedly ungrateful. Also, Ellis has always had things easy and, unlike Mick, finds making money no problem. But most of all, it was Ellis who first introduced Josie to Tony, the man she left Mick for.

One of Ellis's few redeeming features is that he is good with Mick's children, Leo and Gemma. Beneath it all, Ellis has hidden qualities — but for the moment they remain extremely well hidden.

Born in South London, Francis Johnson, who plays his namesake Ellis, trained at the Bristol Old Vic Theatre School. His career leans very much towards the classical, having appeared with the Royal Shakespeare Company in *Romeo and Juliet*, *Cymbeline*, *A Clockwork Orange* and *Faust*, as well as in such productions as *Twelfth Night*, *Macbeth* and *A Midsummer Night's Dream*. He has also written three plays for the stage — *Bad in the Eye*, *A Class of Our Own*, and *Bloody Instructions*. His film work includes *The Tall Guy*.

WHO'S WHO
MICK JOHNSON

Mick Johnson is the Mr. Nice Guy of Brookside Close. He is so amiable that he was in danger of giving taxi drivers a good name. In the back of Mick's cab, you were never subjected to a tirade about the shortcomings of the England football team or the inside story of why Andrew and Fergie split up because Mick had always got enough on his mind.

Abandoned by his wayward wife Josie and left to bring up their two children single-handed, Mick's life has lurched from one crisis to another. While the bills have beeen coming in, his luck's been out.

Actor Louis Emerick is only too aware of the vast wave of public sympathy that exists for Mick. 'People come up to me and say, "When's Mick going to get a bit of good fortune?" And even when his life lightened up a bit and he pulled a pretty girl on a singles' night out with Frank Rogers, what happened? He ended up having to walk Julia Brogan home too. Mick's such a gentleman he wouldn't refuse but it's just his luck after a night out to end up with Julia!

'People used to ask me how Mick put up with Josie — I must say I wouldn't have stood for her behaviour. Then there's Ellis. Mick feels responsible for Ellis but I reckon he's the only one'd stomach him.

'Mick's basically a gentle giant, even-tempered and with endless patience, but I think I'd like to see him go off the rails a bit more. We did see his aggressive side when he lost his rag with Josie over buying knock-off gear and also when he had a go at the burglar who was trying to break into their home. With the burglary, I sympathised with him every inch of the way because I know that, in his position, I would have done exactly the same thing. Mick reacted strongly because it was his children who had been in danger. And all of us would. It's instinct for people to protect their children.'

Liverpool-born Louis was late coming into acting. 'I worked in the car industry first. But I was made redundant from a place in Manchester which made silencers and then another car place, at which I was parts manager, closed down. So there I was in 1983, 30 years old, my wife Mo and three young children to support, and no qualifications. I thought, "What am I going to do?"

'I'd done some amateur dramatics before but, with my responsibilities, I thought at first that acting was a bit too chancy as a career. Anyway, eventually I decided to give it a go and, touch wood, I haven't done too badly. I've been in *Brookside* for three and a half years now which is a nice bit of security.'

Louis Emerick as Mick Johnson.

LEO JOHNSON

Leeon Sawyer as Leo Johnson.

Moving to Brookside Close was a traumatic experience for Gemma's older brother Leo. It soon emerged that he was unhappy at his new school, having been subjected to taunts from his classmates. When Mick confronted the teacher about the problem, he was told that Leo was singled out because he was clever. However Leo was further upset when the teacher cast him as the black king in the school nativity play and it was then that he admitted that some of the remarks directed at him were racist. Leo is a bright lad and is considerably more sensible than, say, Tony Dixon, who is always getting into trouble. He is also a credit to Mick's solo parenthood.

Leo adores his Dad and also loves animals and spent a lot of time helping Mick to search for Harry's dog Monty.

Leo is played by 11-year-old Leeon Sawyer who attends the Richard Gardner Stage School in Liverpool.

WHO'S WHO
GEMMA JOHNSON

Gemma is Mick and Josie Johnson's daughter and, with her mother leaving home yet again but this time for good, she and brother Leo have been cared for by Mick. Their Dad does his best but he has to earn a living and so most of the Close have been called in to lend a hand from time to time. Naturally the children miss out on some treats which Josie's parents were quick to exploit when they hustled them away to Cardiff.

Gemma is naturally playful and inquisitive but those traits brought her a brush with death when she fell into Harry Cross's garden pond and almost died. Only the quick thinking of unlikely hero Geoff Rogers, who administered the kiss of life, saved her. She also gave Mick palpitations when she went missing for a few days before being found safe and well. Gemma is played by six-year-old Naomi Kamanga who, although born in Chester, now lives in Liverpool. *Brookside* is her first taste of television.

Naomi Kamanga as Gemma Johnson.

WHO'S WHO
OWEN DANIELS

I t was a case of third time lucky for Danny McCall when he landed the part of Owen Daniels in *Brookside*. Danny says: 'When they were auditioning right at the start, back in 1982, I heard Phil Redmond on a radio show and wrote off to him. I was shortlisted for the part of Gordon Collins but didn't get it. My mates Shelagh O'Hara and Simon O'Brien were luckier — they were picked to play Karen and Damon Grant.

'Then about six years later, I did appear — as a factory apprentice with Bobby Grant. It was only one episode and any hopes of it running to more than that were dashed when Ricky Tomlinson, who played Bobby, left the show. So my part was written out. Then finally, 12 months later, I was brought back as Owen.'

Owen is the sort of son any parent would be proud of — handsome,

Danny McCall as Owen Daniels.

polite, the original boy next door. Frank and Chrissy Rogers didn't agree about much but one thing they were united in was their approval of Owen as their Sammy's boyfriend.

Owen was in the year above Sammy at *Brookside* Comprehensive and they got together when he hatched an elaborate Valentine's Day plot. The course of true love didn't always run smooth even in those early stages, with Sammy accusing Owen of flirting with her friend Nisha and Owen getting jealous about Sammy's holiday snaps of Luigi. But these were minor hiccups compared to the tragedy of the night out in the stolen car driven by Kav and Tony, which left Owen in a wheelchair.

Racked with guilt because Owen hadn't wanted to get in the car in the first place, Sammy turned to drink. Their relationship went downhill fast. At first Sammy stuck with him, possibly out of pity, but avoided him at every opportunity. In a rare burst of temper, Owen smashed the Rogers' door and thrust a bottle of gin at Sammy, the frigid alcoholic. She promptly told him it was all over.

Then months later, while out with his new girlfriend Grace, he was accosted by a drunken Sammy. Grace responded by throwing her drink over Sammy but even Sammy didn't need that much booze. Gradually they got back together but, after making love on the Sullivans' sofa while the rest of the Close were at the Farnhams' barbecue, Sammy found she was pregnant. Owen was furious but — ever the gentleman — he agreed to do the honourable thing and marry her. To make matters worse, Owen then lost his job. But far from getting any sympathy from his father-in-law, Owen was told by Frank in no uncertain terms to forget about studying for a decent career at college – he had a wife and baby to support. As if the lad needed reminding! Money was tight too – at least when Sammy was drinking they could make a small fortune taking back the empties!

'Poor Owen — he's had a rough time,' says 25-year-old Danny, 'although I'm glad he's hardened up a bit because he was a bit wimpy before. When the writers decided to end the relationship two years ago, I thought that was the last we'd see of Owen. But when they brought him back, I was really pleased because I missed working on *Brookside*.'

Like a number of the *Brookside* cast, Danny trained at the Elliot Clarke Theatre School in Liverpool. Among his stage roles has been that of sixties' rock star Rory Storm in *The Need For Heroes*, while on television he starred in the Channel Four film *Borrowed Time* and played a postman in two episodes of *Bread*. 'I delivered the giros to the Boswells.'

Both off and on screen, the love of Danny's life is Rachael Lindsay who plays Sammy. 'I reckon I can pinpoint the exact moment when Rachael fell for me,' he laughs. 'I remember it vividly. She came to see me in pantomime, took one look at me in my Dick Whittington jodhpurs and that was it. Neither of us has ever looked back since!'

How did Danny react to Sammy's love affair with Tim? 'It was horrendous. It made me sick to watch this old man with Owen's girlfriend. I wanted to kill him. Then I met Tim's actor, Christopher Blake, and to my horror and amazement, he turned out to be a great guy and I felt no venom towards him at all.

'The character of Owen seems to be really popular with teenage girls. I think it stems from the time when Sammy was treating him badly — they all feel a bit sorry for him. So do I sometimes because I don't think I would put up with Sammy. And I certainly could never have lived under the same roof as Frank!'

WHO'S WHO
SAMMY DANIELS

Rachael Lindsay as Sammy Daniels.

Sammy's been through a lot of ups and downs,' laments 20-year-old Rachael Lindsay. 'Personally, I don't think I could have coped with what she's been through.

Nor could many girls. In her short life, Sammy has been in a fatal car crash, which left her boyfriend in a coma; hit the bottle; been involved in a bitter relationship with an older man; seen her Mum leave home on her wedding day; and had to cope with the pressures of being a young Mum herself. It's tough being a teenager in a soap.

Rachael's enthusiasm for acting began at an early age. 'At school, drama was a lesson like any other subject, and I just took to it. Also, my sister Nikki is a drama teacher so I suppose I followed her interest. I appeared in various school productions and then I heard about

Brookside auditioning for this new family, the Rogers. I got the part of Sammy when I was 15 and still at school. I had watched *Brookside* before and I'd always liked it.'

Sammy's trials and tribulations have meant that Rachael has received a mixed reaction from viewers. 'Sometimes the public really like her and feel for her, other times they hate her and think she's a horrid cow. In the beginning, Sammy was rebellious and headstrong and all for animal rights and I really liked her — she knew what she wanted. I was particularly glad we did the alcoholism story because it can happen to anyone — like you'd have thought Sammy was too sensible to have got in a mess like that. I didn't do any research as such because I didn't feel I had the right to go round to people and ask: "Oh and what was it like when you were an alcoholic?" I wanted to do it properly and it was a real challenge. What I didn't want was for Sammy to be laughed at — just to go around giggling and falling off stools.

'I've been lucky because I've dealt with such powerful subjects. In one role, I've experienced things that some actresses don't get to do in their whole career. I've gone from schoolgirl to wife to mother.'

Rachael believes that her close relationship with Danny McCall enhances their on-screen scenes. 'We actually worked together for a whole year before we started going out. It was one of those things — we just clicked. Because Danny and I feel comfortable with each other, we can even handle the scenes where Sammy and Owen argue. We help each other out. And no matter how much we fall out on screen, it doesn't affect us as a couple.'

WHO'S WHO
KATIE ROGERS

Even her best friends couldn't describe Katie Rogers as happy-go-lucky. But then again, she hasn't had a lot to laugh about. Katie is a very intense girl who feels deeply about everything and, like most teenagers, is more concerned with the state of the world than the state of her bedroom.

At first, she was more outgoing but then a school bully named Bagga started picking on her because she was intelligent and popular. The evil Bagga forced Katie to steal money and the problem was only resolved when Sammy, Geoff and his pal Bumper Humphries ambushed her on the Close.

Katie then developed a crush on science teacher Mr. Molyneaux and to impress him, decided to clean up a nearby river with the help of her friends Siobhan and Jenny. Unfortunately, Katie fell in the polluted water and was rushed to hospital suffering from a form of toxaemia.

But understandably, Katie's greatest heartache was over her parents' separation. She desperately wanted to keep them together, and couldn't believe that Chrissy would ever really leave. For all their problems, they were a family – and that's how Katie wanted them to stay. She didn't understand why they were drifting apart – after all, it wasn't her fault that her parents argued constantly. She has had a rough time since their split, falling under the bad influence of school friend Leanne Powell, who made a play for Owen, and then falling out with Frank over his friendship with Denise. Katie wasn't ready for anyone to take her mum's place.

Sixteen-year-old Diane Burke became the second Katie Rogers in December 1988. She lives in Huyton and is a former pupil at Liverpool's Knowsley Hey School. Diane, who is also a keen dancer, says: 'I first became interested in drama when I played the leading role in a school production of Cinderella. I enjoyed it so much that my drama teacher encouraged me to pursue an acting career and I found myself being invited to audition for *Brookside*.'

Diane Burke as Katie Rogers.

WHO'S WHO
FRANK ROGERS

Some people think that the only place you can get a bigger divvy than Frank Rogers is at the Co-op. He can be impetuous, chauvinistic and narrow-minded — and those are his good points. The only thing that is articulate about him is his lorry.

Forty-five-year-old Liverpool actor Peter Christian concedes: 'It's true he upsets a lot of people — he tends to jump in with both feet — and he can be hard work to live with, but his heart's in the right place. He's got a lot on his plate, particularly since Chrissy left, but he's a good

Peter Christian as Frank Rogers.

family man. And he thinks the world of his kids.

'The thing with Frank is he's set in his ways. He wanted his kids disciplined the way he was brought up and that was always a problem with Chrissy. He felt Chrissy's place was at home with the kids, not out at work. The reason he was mortified over the business with Tim was because he was so close to Sammy. That was a classic example of how he jumped in — as far as Frank was concerned, that relationship was wrong. If he had listened to Chrissy, he'd have let them carry on. So Frank was right over that one.'

Whatever his faults, Frank does only want the best for his children although sometimes his principles get in the way. When Chrissy wanted Geoff to seek private medical help for his dyslexia, Frank strongly disagreed because of his Socialist principles and the benefits of the NHS. In the end, he gave in. Peter says: 'Chrissy was the one who was educated, Frank used to back down for the sake of peace. Blokes claim in the pub that they're the boss at home, but actually in the house, they go for the quiet life.'

Frank and Chrissy had been married for nearly 19 years when she walked out to go to teacher's training college. She wanted to broaden her horizons. She felt she had outgrown Frank, particularly after meeting up again with her old student friend Gina Phillips. Frank was left with the kids and his memories of the Scotty Dogs, the band he used to play with in the sixties who were responsible for such gems as *Nobody Butters The Toast Like You.* Now Frank had to learn how the toaster worked.

Peter Christian, who is married

*Billy J. Kramer tells Frank Rogers
(Peter Christian) why The Scotty
Dogs never made the big time.*

and lives on the Wirral, got into acting by accident. 'I used to do all sorts of jobs. I went to sea, I worked for the Forestry Commission, I got jobs on building sites and I worked on the docks, driving a lorry just like Frank.

'I was working on a building site when a cousin of mine, who was into amateur dramatics, asked me to go along one night to help shift scenery at the little David Lewis Theatre in Liverpool. The upshot of it was that I was asked whether I'd take a small part in the following week's production.

'Soon I started to think of acting as an alternative to labouring. I thought, "Shall I have a go or regret it for the rest of my life?" So I decided to give it a bash.'

He made his stage debut in *Her Benny* and went on to appear in *Look Back In Anger*, Dennis Potter's *Son of Man*, and as Zigger in the football drama *Zigger Zagger*. His television credits include *Boys From The Blackstuff*, *Scully*, *The Brothers MacGregor*, and *Travelling Man*.

'I also played a character called Horse in the BBC series *Truckers*. I honestly don't know whether that led directly to the role of lorry-driver Frank in *Brookside* but I do know that, one way or another, trucks have played a major part in my life.'

RON DIXON

Vince Earl has seen it all in showbusiness. He's literally given the Beatles a helping hand, seen his hopes of stardom crushed by a cross-eyed stuffed bear and, as a comic, has died a death in some of Britain's most notorious clubs. After all that, he can cope with anything that Maxie Farnham might throw at him.

Liverpool-born Vince started out as a singer when he was 11. 'I was around before the Beatles but later I often appeared on the same bill as them. In those days, they had this old Morris van and I can still remember the night it broke down after a gig in Birkenhead when my group, Vince Earl and the Zeros, were playing with them. We had to give them a push to get the van going!'

When Vince joined Rory Storm and The Hurricanes, he also appeared with the Fab Four at the famous Star Club in Hamburg. 'Ringo Starr had just left Rory to play with the Beatles and our name was in big letters at the top of the posters. In little blocks underneath they had people like the Beatles and Billy J. Kramer. It's a bit sad because all the other acts made it right to the top but Rory didn't.'

In the seventies, fronting the Vince Earl Attraction on New Faces, Vince was beaten into second place by the redoubtable Roger de Courcey and Nookie Bear. In 1977, Vince left the Attraction to pursue a solo career as a comedian. 'After so long, keeping a band on the road was uneconomical so I went solo. But having had your own group, it was frustrating being backed by club bands and so I started cracking gags. Added to which, comedians make more money than singers.'

Television work followed, including *The Comedians*, *Starburst* and *The Video Entertainers*, as well as a few dates Vince would rather forget. 'The worst one was at a club in Middlesbrough called Brambles Farm British Legion. It was a Tuesday night and there was a cover charge put on the door because they said the artist was on VAT. I don't know whether it was that which upset them or not. I tried everything. Ten minutes of gags — nothing. So I got the band and you can really sing when you're dying. Still nothing. Total silence. I was on for 40 minutes in all and it seemed like three weeks.

'Some of those places were amazing. I've had concert secretaries call me over half-way through my act and whisper, "Pssst. Get off. You're crap." Another time, the secretary came on, grabbed the microphone and announced to the audience: "Excuse me, there's a car blocking the entrance. Can you move it please. And now on with the act." How do you follow that? All you can do is make a gag about it.'

Vince's third metamorphosis was into actor. He appeared in Alan Bleasdale's *Boys From The Blackstuff* and *No Surrender* before landing the role of Ron Dixon.

Ron first arrived in *Brookside* as a cross between Jed Clampett and Captain Ahab. He had been foreman at a local factory for years before using his redundancy money to start up his ramshackle mobile shop, known to all and sundry as The Moby. He proceeded to park this splendid vehicle in his front drive, to the horror of the Farnhams. It's one thing being close to the shops, but another thing having them practically in your hallway. But in 1991,

Vince Earl as Ron Dixon.

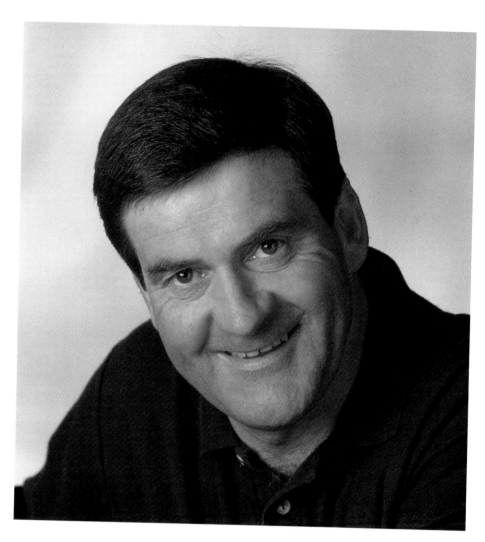

ever on the lookout for business expansion, he moved up in the world with his own shop.

'Ron always wanted the shop,' says Vince, 'but he still feels a great sense of loyalty to The Moby, not only because that's where it all started but also because that's another way of making money.

'He's basically a well-meaning fellow but he has certain ethics that he believes are right. He works hard and is a very devoted Dad but sometimes he feels his kids aren't giving him as much as they should. He just wants them to succeed in life. Really, his aim is to earn a living and to let everyone live their own lives.

'The one person he doesn't see eye to eye with is Max Farnham. He sees Max as a bit pompous — he reckons life's come a bit too easy for Max. Maybe Ron's a bit resentful. But he certainly doesn't think Max contributes enough to the Close because — let's be honest — Max just looks after himself.'

Vince, 44, can identify with Ron in many respects. 'I moan at my kids about money in the same way as Ron moans at his. I've got three kids at home (Kimberley, 12, Stephen, 15, and Nicole, 18) — the same as Ron. My wife's name is Irene and my screen wife DD is played by Irene Marot. And just as Ron has his shop, so my Irene owns a newsagent's in the Wirral. I'm glad it ends there, though, and that I don't have to swap my Mercedes for The Moby!'

WHO'S WHO

DD DIXON

Debbie Dixon, known to all as DD, has taken over from Sheila Grant as the Close's religious zealot. She had an unhappy time as a teenager, both her parents dying when she was 17. Her father died from a terminal illness and her mother committed suicide shortly afterwards.

At the time of this double tragedy, DD was a novice nun, having just left convent school, and its effect was to make her strongly question her faith. If there is a God, then how can He let such things happen?

Turning her back on her belief, DD left the convent, intent on living life to the full. She indulged in a period of wild sprees, 'clubbing' it for eight months.

Irene Marot as DD Dixon.

Then it all came to an abrupt end when she suffered a nervous breakdown, caused by the onset of grief and guilt about losing both her parents and her faith. She admitted herself voluntarily into a mental institution as an in-patient and stayed there for 18 months.

When she was in hospital, she met Maria Benson who was working there as a cleaner and they formed a close friendship. When she had recovered, DD began to rebuild her life and 20 years ago she married Ron. For years, she never told Ron about her time either in the convent or in hospital. Fearing his reaction, she invented a totally new past for herself. Only Maria knew, but DD's loyalty to her friend was tested to the limit when Maria embarked on an affair. DD found herself having to lie to Maria's husband Charlie — something she hated doing. Ron hated her doing it too and it was then that DD finally told him about her secret past.

DD's traumatic history undoubt-edly accounted for her ferocious opposition to the relationship between her younger brother Derek and Margaret. Actress Irene Marot says: 'DD is certainly over-protective towards Derek — I think it's bringing up her own guilt from the past. I know one thing, DD's more fun to play than when she first came in and was very nice, just a mediator in Dixon family squabbles.'

Irene, who is not a Catholic, was born in Birkenhead although she now lives in London. 'I always wanted to be an actress — I remember putting on shows as a child and doing plays in the local church hall. I went on to study drama at teacher training college and I taught drama in Margate for a year.'

Irene reveals that she was nearly Doreen Corkhill in *Brookside*. 'I auditioned for Doreen but didn't get it. I think they remembered me when it came to casting for DD. And, in spite of DD's problems, I think I'm better off with the Dixons!'

MIKE DIXON

Brookside is like a family affair for the Byatts. For 20-year-old Paul Byatt, who plays Mike Dixon, is the fifth member of the talented family to appear in the show.

Paul says: 'Years ago, my sister Jane and brother Liam played a couple of kids, then my sister Sharon was Jonathan Gordon-Davies's secretary Coral, my other sister Michelle is Tracy Corkhill's pal Nikki White — and finally, there's me. Turning out cast members for *Brookside* is almost a family industry!'

A former pupil of Liverpool's St. Edwards College, Paul worked as an usher at the city's Playhouse Theatre and trained with the Liverpool Playhouse Youth Theatre. After his 'A' Levels, he continued the family tradition by auditioning for *Brookside*.

'I'd often watched *Brookside* and I really loved it when it was first on. It was like a breath of fresh air.'

Mike Dixon first appeared as a streetwise but likeable youth. His main interest was music, and forming his own rock band. 'He was OK,' says Paul, 'and next to someone like Sinnott, he appeared an angel. But then he started robbing from his Dad.'

First it was money from the Trading Post till, for which he framed poor Julia Brogan, and then he pinched the late Cyril's war medals. That was too much for Ron and after a scuffle, he threw Mike out. Worse still, Mike discovered that Ron had unwittingly become an organ donor.

'The trouble with Mike is that he thinks he's clever — he reckons he knows more than his Dad,' says Paul. 'He also thinks he can fend for himself but he can't. And he hasn't a clue about money. That's how he got himself into debt with his credit card, when he bought that electric organ, and that's why he had to start stealing.

'I certainly wouldn't have got away with half of the things Mike did. Long before Ron finally took action, my Dad would have sorted me out if I'd behaved anything like Mike. I'd probably have ended up with two black eyes, a broken nose and a broken jaw!'

Paul Byatt as Mike Dixon.

Alexandra Fletcher as Jackie Dixon.

Blazing satchels! Jackie Dixon is trapped in the school fire.

Maybe because she's a good swimmer, Jackie Dixon isn't averse to pulling a few strokes. Cheeky Jackie is independent and extremely self-reliant and tends to keep apart from her brothers, Mike and Tony.

Sadly, her single-mindedness sometimes lands her in trouble. She has had regular bust-ups with her parents, including the time the police arrested her for being in possession of acid, the row over her demands for a pair of £70 trainers and also when she defied Ron's orders forbidding her to see Darren Murphy. Instead, she joined Darren's gang as they broke into Manor Park Primary School but when a fire started accidentally, she had to be rescued from the inferno by the passing Barry Grant. But despite her apparent cockiness, her vulnerability showed when Darren threatened her to keep quiet about the fire. She felt helpless and didn't know what to do until she finally blurted out the truth to Barbara Harrison. Jackie was at last forced to admit that this was one situation she couldn't handle. But although she had to rely on an adult to bail her out of trouble, it seems doubtful whether the experience will result in her having any greater respect for her parents.

'Jackie never seems to learn.' Admits sixteen-year-old Alexandra Fletcher: 'First it was drugs, then Darren. But I believe her weakness reflects real life. Some girls are attracted to wild boys. Darren was one of the hard lads and dead popular because of it. The unfortunate truth is that girls like Jackie do go for that type.'

Alexandra, whose other television experience includes the children's programme *Why Don't You...?* for the BBC and BSB's *Cool Cube*, was on holiday with a friend's family at Butlin's in Pwllheli when she was called to return to *Brookside* to read again for Jackie Dixon. 'My parents dashed to North Wales to fetch me,' says Alexandra, 'but it was well worth the effort and I didn't really mind the disruption to my holiday. Getting the part of Jackie was a dream come true.'

Disco-loving Alexandra attends the ART Drama Studio where she is a student of Nikki Lindsay, sister of Rachael who plays *Brookside*'s Sammy Daniels.

WHO'S WHO

TONY DIXON

The youngest of the Dixon clan but, in terms of nuisance value, he's able to hold his own with the best. Tony gave a hint of the future parental joys in store for Ron and DD when, on his seventh birthday, he drank half a bottle of Martini and had to have his stomach pumped. He hasn't looked back since.

When the Dixons first moved in, if there was mischief afoot on the Close, the chances were that Tony and his mates Togga and Benno were behind it. He revelled in the Dixons' hostilities with the Farnhams, first arranging a delivery of ten pizzas to Max, then sending Patricia 15 Valentine's cards complete with poems, and finally masterminding the collapse of the Farnhams' shed. And Tony thought nothing of sneaking a look at an erotic video. Ron didn't think much of it either and grounded him.

Considered something of a hero at school, Tony is a pain to the rest of his family, not least because he supports Liverpool and the rest follow Everton. Tony Dixon just has to be different.

The second Tony Dixon (succeeding Gerard Bostock) is 13-year-old Mark Lennock who lives across the Mersey in Bebington on the Wirral and attends Wirral Grammar School. *Brookside* marks his first television appearance.

Mark Lennock as Tony Dixon.

WHO'S WHO
DEREK O'FARRELL

At one stage, Clive Moore thought he would be spending the rest of his life looking into people's mouths. But then he decided to look into acting instead and ended up landing his first major television role as turbulent priest Derek O'Farrell in *Brookside*.

'I spent two years training as a dentist,' says Clive. 'But I realised I wouldn't be very good at it and decided that acting looked more interesting.'

Having made up his mind to swap molars for *Macbeth*, Birkenhead-born Clive, who is 28, single and lives in Manchester, studied at Manchester Polytechnic for three years and left in 1990 after achieving a diploma in Theatre. Prior to joining *Brookside*, Clive's experience had been limited to Theatre in Education projects among Cheshire schools. But his sensitive portrayal of the tormented Derek has earned him praise from press and priests alike. And that is no mean feat, dealing with such a delicate subject as religion.

'I'm not a Catholic myself,' says Clive, 'so in order to research the role thoroughly, I had to speak to a number of priests. I found them extremely helpful and I must say talking to them helped me to sympathise with Derek's situation. At first, he was struggling mentally, nervously kidding himself about his feelings. He simply couldn't make up his mind. But then he realised that he had to face the truth — that Margaret was more than a friend.

'Although I accept that a priest should give his whole life to God, I think it's a great shame that it has to be like that. Priests themselves

Clive Moore as Derek O'Farrell.

have admitted to me that they're only human.'

Derek, the younger brother of DD Dixon, first appeared as a shy, unworldly young man who didn't seem in the least bit interested in responding to the infatuation of the equally innocent Margaret. To him, she was little more than a potential helper, someone who was good with children and might therefore be useful on church outings. If their friendship continued, he probably saw her graduating to dried flower arranging or, at best, to running the tombola stall at the spring fête. However, a brief but intimate Christmas kiss changed all that and the great love story began – and Derek had to face a different kind of fate.

WHO'S WHO
MARGARET CLEMENCE

Nicola Stephenson as Margaret Clemence.

When Margaret Clemence left her native Oldham to become the Farnhams' live-in nanny, it was partly to escape from her over-powering boyfriend Kieran who was keen to get engaged. But it was a case of out of the frying pan, into the fire as she soon became besotted with young priest Derek O'Farrell and started nibbling away at the forbidden fruit. In her early days on the Close, it seemed that Margaret was going to become romantically involved with Mike Dixon but any interest there rapidly fizzled out. She then turned her attentions to Derek.

At first, Derek considered her to be just a friend but as she grew more persistent, travelling miles to see him in his parish, he realised

that he felt the same way. The Farnhams arranged clandestine meetings for them but the opposition, in the ferocious shape of Derek's sister DD and Margaret's mum, were determined to put a stop to the relationship. In the end, though, young love won through – after a few awkward moments when Margaret attempted to pursuade Derek to swap the Bible for the Kama Sutra.

DD was adamant that Margaret was totally to blame for chasing after Derek but 21-year-old Nicola Stephenson, who plays Margaret, sees two points of view. 'I used to feel very sorry for Derek because he didn't ask for this extremely naive girl to fall in love with him. But then he didn't do much to discourage her in the early stages of their relationship either. He was awfully friendly towards Margaret, and became quite flirtatious during one episode when he came in for coffee and helped her dry the pots. Her previous boyfriend was always trying it on with her and she wouldn't let him come near but she felt safe with Derek, knowing he was a man of the cloth.

'It's absolutely believable that she'd end up falling for him but I didn't know that he was going to fall in love with her as well — the Producer didn't tell me that!

'I must admit I was a bit apprehensive about the storyline at first but it's been a really good issue to cover and one that's never been done before. I had a lot of reaction and all the letters I received were positive — people said they wanted Margaret and Derek to get together.

'A priest isn't deprived of natural male feelings. One I know of actually said he looks at girls and thinks

"very nice", but he realises he can't touch and that's the end of the story.'

Nicola's interest in acting started at North Chadderton School in Oldham. 'I appeared in almost all of the school plays and joined the Oldham Theatre Workshop when I was 12. When I left school, my former classmates and I founded our own theatre group, The Increasingly Important Theatre Company. We've performed at places like the Oldham Coliseum, The Green Room in Manchester, the Edinburgh Festival and the National Students' Drama Festival.'

This is Nicola's first major TV role although she has previously appeared in the popular series *Children's Ward* and the Channel Four film *The Final Frame*.

But there has been another casualty of Margaret's fling with Derek — little Thomas Farnham, the boy she is supposed to be minding. 'I'm afraid Margaret did rather neglect Thomas,' confesses Nicola, 'so much so that she nearly got the sack. The little lad, whose real name is Mark, is smashing as long as his Mum is close by. And he always calls me Margaret. I'm used to children because, although I'm an only child, I've got lots of younger cousins whom I've known since they were babies.

'Margaret has certainly grown up a lot since she moved in with the Farnhams. And do you know what I like best about it all? She's remained a really nice girl.'

Derek and Margaret.

WHO'S WHO
MAX FARNHAM

'**M**ax is a victim of unfortunate circumstances,' states actor Steven Pinder. 'He has seemingly endless money problems — what with paying off his first wife Susannah, two kids from the previous marriage, two mortgages, two cars and he has to pay for the nanny. That's why he and Patricia both have to work. Max met Susannah when they were both sixth formers studying for their 'A' Levels. They married immediately after taking their exams and moving on to Liverpool Polytechnic. However, Susannah soon became pregnant and her parents had to subsidise them, but no sooner had they settled into their first house than Susannah announced that she was pregnant again. It was becoming a habit and marked the beginning of the end of their relationship. Soon Max found himself having an affair with Patricia.

With a power of fertility that would make him a God in some countries, Max immediately proceeded to get Patricia pregnant too. A bitter divorce with Susannah ensued. Max's maintenance payments were crippling and even with his salary as a quantity surveyor, he and Patricia realised they would have to move into a small, three-bedroomed house to give their son Thomas a garden to play in. And so they moved to *Brookside* Close and found themselves next door to the Dixons.

'The relationship with the Dixons was always bad,' says Steven, 'but it got worse with the problems over Margaret and Derek. It was like one of the Montagues going off with one of the Capulets — only worse because he was a priest.

Born in Whalley, Lancashire, Steven became involved in amateur dramatics through the teachers at school. He joined Manchester Youth Theatre then went to Drama Centre in London for three years. 'My first break was in *Macbeth* at the Shaw Theatre — I played the Third Witch.

'My TV debut was in a commercial for Bonusprint.'

Subsequent roles brought him slightly nearer home for the comedy series *Foxy Lady*, the action adventure *CATS Eyes*, and the incomparable *Crossroads*. 'I played Roy Lambert, the shop owner who broke the heart of the lovely Anne-Marie Wade, played by Dee Hepburn.'

When the opportunity arose to appear in a second soap, Steven didn't hesitate. 'I'd always admired *Brookside* and I'd never played a character quite like Max before.'

Steven Pinder as Max Farnham.

PATRICIA FARNHAM

As she was wheeled into the operating theatre for Patricia Farnham's breast cancer operation, Gabrielle Glaister admits that she was nearly in tears. But they were tears of laughter at the absurdity of the situation.

Gabrielle explains: 'When we shot that scene of me being wheeled into the theatre, we should have had a Stedicam going with us, filming Steven Pinder as Max walking along beside me, holding my hand. But the camera broke. It was late and we were going into overtime but we wanted to get that scene finished. So for those shots, we had a cameraman sitting on the trolley with me, holding a camera above me, and Steven on the other end of the trolley leaning on his back to get into shot. So, instead of just me, there were three of us on this trolley. It was hysterical.'

Prior to her illness, Patricia had appeared very much the career woman, relishing her job as an accounts executive for a high-powered international advertising agency based in Manchester. 'Patricia seemed snotty but I don't think she was,' says Gabrielle. 'Some people have that manner, which can be slightly misleading. It is difficult to make a career happen when you're a mother too so sometimes she had to be single-minded and it made her appear sharp. Also, she was defensive and guilty about leaving Thomas to go out to work and about taking Max from Susannah.'

Born in Moreton-in-Marsh in the heart of the Cotswolds, Gabrielle studied English and drama at Chichester College and subsequently trained at the National Youth Theatre. Her TV debut was in an episode of *Jury* and she went on to appear in *Grange Hill* (as a young mum), *Rockliffe's Babies*, *Blackadder II*, *Happy Families*, *Wish Me Luck*, and many more.

'Four years ago, I also did an episode of *Casualty* in which I played someone with a lump on her breast. There's obviously something about me...'

Gabrielle, who lives in North London with her boyfriend, confesses that once on *Brookside*, the tears were for real. 'Our nanny Margaret was supposed to be doing a crying scene for which they use menthol crystals to induce the tears. Unfortunately, the make-up lady accidentally dropped the crystals in the room and everybody had to go outside weeping!'

Gabrielle Glaister as Patricia Farnham.

WHO'S WHO
TERRY SULLIVAN

Time was when Terry Sullivan wouldn't say boo to a goose. Now he'd probably systematically pluck it and have it for lunch. For Terry is a changed man and one person who has been revelling in his new-found notoriety is actor Brian Regan.

'The character has definitely changed for the better,' says Brian. 'He used to be Mr. Dependable, always wanting to settle down and have a family. But when he found out that Danny wasn't his, he flipped. Then after the murder, for the first time in his life he had money to spend. So he started drinking a lot, trying to blot out the past. It's a great character for me to play because he's been through so many different emotions.'

Terry made his debut way back in episode six. 'The early days were great fun,' enthuses Brian. 'There was a rawness about *Brookside* — it was exciting. I used to enjoy the scams that Barry and Terry got up to — the best one was when we left the car to drown on the beach. Terry was more sensible than Barry. He was a bit cowardly really and wouldn't take as many chances as Barry. Paul Usher and I were always called the terrible twins because we got on right from the moment we first met.'

What sort of reaction did Brian get to the murder of Sue and Danny? 'People knew it couldn't have been Terry,' says Brian. 'They didn't think

The distraught Terry Sullivan receives a helping hand from his Dad Jack.

Terry was capable of doing it. They always said they thought it was Barry.' Even so, Brian is still unable to account for his alter ego's precise whereabouts on the day of the crime. 'Terry knew Sue had done it once before with Martin, now he thought she was at it again with Graeme and that was enough for him. So he just went off and got drunk somewhere.

'I don't want Terry to settle down into family life again just yet. If he does, he'll have all the traumas of a relationship. I'd like him to have a bit of luck, not to always be down in the dumps, whingeing about having no money. I'd like to see him enjoying himself. Above all, it would be nice to see him smile.'

Before acting, Brian had a different goal — one he kept each week as a schoolboy with Liverpool Football Club. 'I was 16 when I joined Liverpool — Ray Clemence was first-team keeper at the time. I stayed two years before I decided to pack it in. At the back of my mind, I'd always wanted to act, having been in various school plays, and anyway my Dad said the decision was entirely up to me. I've no regrets about packing in football. I was lucky in that while I was there, I fulfilled a lot of youngsters' dreams by meeting and training with Bill Shankly and playing at Anfield.'

Brian started out as an Assistant Stage Manager with Liverpool Playhouse and stayed with the company for seven years. One of his first TV roles was the children's drama series *Murphy's Mob*, set at a football club. And, surprise surprise, Brian was chosen to play goalkeeper Stevie King. 'We filmed it at Watford FC,' recalls Brian, 'and I think when they first saw me, the Watford players thought, "typical actor". But after I'd pulled off a few smart saves, particularly a penalty rebound from Luther Blissett, they treated me with more respect and started taking shots at me.

Brian Regan as Terry Sullivan.

'While I was appearing in *Stags and Hens* at Liverpool Playhouse, I auditioned for *Brookside*... as Barry Grant. That was in the May and I never heard anything until the August. I was then told that I'd got a screen test but again I didn't hear anything for six or seven weeks. Finally, I got a phone call to say, "You didn't get the part of Barry but you've got his best mate, Terry." In the end, it's worked out just as well.'

Brian, still resides in Liverpool and for the past three years has been married to Lisa, who has been with *Brookside* since 1983 and is now the secretary of *Brookside* Producer Mal Young. Brian and Lisa have a two-year-old daughter Ashleigh Gemma.

Tony Scoggins as Matty Nolan.

Tony Scoggins was recently enjoying a quiet Saturday evening meal at home when he heard an almighty crash outside. 'I looked out and there were four cars at different angles, one virtually through our garden wall. I phoned the police and we ran out with towels to see what we could do. There were a lot of injuries. One car had two young lads in it and one of them had clearly broken his jaw — there was blood everywhere. I said to this kid, "Hold this towel." Just then, he looked up and said: "Bloody 'ell, how're you doin', Matty?" It was amazing. In the middle of all this blood, the only thing this kid could think about was that he'd met Matty off *Brookside*.'

Matty has been in *Brookside* intermittently since the very first week back in 1982. 'I went for the part of Bobby Grant and got Matty as a consolation.' But Tony got a further, less pleasant, reminder of the character's impact when Matty was a prime suspect in the rape of Sheila Grant.

'It was while the rape story was going and I was getting off the train at Euston Station. This bunch of schoolgirls shouted out, "There's Matty" and made a grab for me!'

Born in the heart of Liverpool's dockland, Tony discovered his flair for showbusiness while at sea. He spent 12 years at sea working for the Cunard Cruise Line in the catering division, and after hours he entertained the crew on the guitar. He returned to Liverpool in 1963 and played the club circuit in various bands. In one band, Wooden Nickel, he teamed up with Ricky Tomlinson, later to play Matty's best mate, Bobby Grant, in *Brookside*.

'They were terrific days — we were doing the circuit at the same time as people like Gerry and the Pacemakers. And I'll never forget the Walton Trades and Labour Club, mainly because we always had to carry the equipment up four flights of stairs.

'In 1970, I got itchy feet and returned to sea with the Norwegian Caribbean Cruise Line but a year later I was back in Liverpool as a community officer, helping ex-offenders. In fact, I was still doing that work while I was appearing in *Brookside*.'

Tony's many roles include *Give Us A Break*, *Albion Market*, *Dr. Who* and, most recently, Freddie Boswell in the national stage tour of *Bread*. At 57, and with four children and six grandchildren, Tony's life is as full as ever.

WHO'S WHO
ANGELA LAMBERT

Hilary Welles will never forget the day she landed the part of hairdresser Angela Lambert in *Brookside* — it meant she didn't have to go back to her temporary job as a waitress.

'I'd really only been waitressing because I was bored and I was working at this restaurant in the City of London. I went up to Liverpool for the audition for *Brookside* and afterwards I was very nervous waiting at my Mum's to hear. But that afternoon my agent rang me back and said, "You've got the part. You don't have to go back to London."

'I was supposed to be waitressing there the next day so it was wonderful to be able to ring up the restaurant and say, "I'm awfully sorry but *Brookside* want me..." I don't think they were too pleased.'

Hilary was born in Huyton and did a degree at Manchester in media and theatre before doing fringe acting around Liverpool. She went to drama school in London, at the Webber Douglas, and made her television debut in *Bread* as Jack Boswell's girlfriend Rachel Byron. *Brookside* is her second TV role.

'Angie is a very strong character,' says Hilary. 'She has to be — she's got two children and, until the armed robbery, ran the hairdressing salon. After she split up from her husband Colin, she realised she could stand on her own two feet. With Barry and Angie, it was a battle of wills. She didn't want him to walk all over her. Barry found that Angie was the first woman he'd fancied who was more interested in business than being with him. He may be a very cool guy but Angie can be equally cool. He'd met his match.

'Personally, I wouldn't trust Barry Grant an inch. He's not my kind of guy but I can appreciate the sex appeal of someone who keeps you on the run.'

How did Hilary cope with the crimping? 'My friend Sylvia is a hairdresser and she does my hair so I watched her and picked up a few tips. I also spent a day at a hairdressing school by way of research but it was hard to look professional, doing hair properly and acting at the same time. So I tried to keep it simple, checking and saying, "That looks nice," rather than having to put in perm rollers. If anyone came in wanting a perm, forget it! I must confess I'd never harboured any secret ambitions to be a hairdresser — it always seemed like hard work to me, standing up all day.'

Hilary, who is single and lives in Islington, North London, should certainly be able to outwit Barry. She is an accomplished chess player and was chess captain at school. But whatever the future holds, Hilary is certain of one thing. 'I've vowed never to go back to waitressing.'

Hilary Welles as Angela Lambert.

WHO'S WHO
BARBARA HARRISON

I t was almost inevitable that Angela Morant would become an actress. 'I think it was hoped that I would become a doctor but I come from a very theatrical background. My father Philip Morant was in *The Archers* for years and my brother Richard and sister Jane are both well-known actors. I remember when I was young going to see my father on stage and thinking that it was absolutely wonderful. So from then on, I'm afraid it was definitely acting for me.'

Raised in Warwickshire, Angela has appeared in a string of productions since leaving drama school including, on stage, *Hedda Gabler*, *The Glass Menagerie* and *The Doll's House* and, on television, *I Claudius*, *Bergerac* and *Inspector Morse*. 'Years ago, I was also in an episode of *Coronation Street* as a marriage guidance counsellor trying to sort out the problems of Emily and Ernest Bishop.'

The Harrisons are outsiders in the Close but Barbara, as Deputy Headmistress at Brookside

Peter Harrison (Robert Beck) rescues mum Barbara (Angela Morant) from the unwelcome attentions of Darren Murphy and his gang.

Comprehensive, soon found that home life and school life have a nasty habit of overlapping – particularly when you live in the same road as some of the pupils. It was like The Sheriff of Nottingham moving in next door to the Merrie Men.

Angela says: 'When Chrissy Rogers walked out on her family, it left young Katie with particular problems connected with growing up. For example, Katie had a party and her friends tried to make her go into the bedroom and kiss the boys but Katie resisted and ran out of the house. Seeing her in distress, Barbara tried to help and it was the beginning of a relationship where I offered her an auntie's shoulder to cry on in place of Chrissy's.'

Then of course, Barbara's intervention in the school break-in prompted brutal retaliation from Darren's gang which ultimately involved the entire Close. 'Some people might argue that the Harrisons were foolish to live that near to the school,' says Angela, 'but remember they were on a limited income. And it's quite apparent that Barbara is not a home person — she doesn't enjoy cooking — so she wanted somewhere that wasn't too big and didn't require a lot of cleaning.'

With two grown-up children of her own, Angela has had plenty of experience with teachers. 'In many ways, acting is like teaching in that we both try to communicate, get ideas across to people, but teaching is a far more difficult job. It's amazing the way teachers can stand up in front of a class — a captive audience so to speak — and command attention. I think they do marvellous jobs — they're very dedicated and don't get the credit they deserve.'

Angela Morant as Barbara Harrison.

WHO'S WHO
JOHN HARRISON

Geoffrey Leesley was left with mixed feelings the day his role as Detective Super-intendent Frank Mathews in Mersey Television's police series *Waterfront Beat* came to an end.

· 'I enjoyed playing Frank and feel that it was a shame the BBC dropped it when they did. After two series, we'd done the hard work and were beginning to pick up a steady audience. Anyway, we all received a letter from Phil Redmond informing us of the bad news but at the bottom of mine, it said: "How do you fancy coming to do something in *Brookside*? We could use you."

Geoffrey Leesley as John Harrison.

'I didn't need much persuading because I've always liked *Brookside* even though, at 8pm, it did tend to clash with the children's bedtime.'

John Harrison had taken early retirement after he and his older brother Hugh closed down their engineering firm which manufac-tured brass pins for electrical plugs. John was Production Manager and Hugh was in charge of the financial side. The reason behind John's deci-sion to get out was that he suffered from late-onset asthma. Hugh went off to Spain and John put his money into savings, only to be shattered by the revelation that he could lose everything because Hugh had been fiddling the VAT.

'That was just one of John's prob-lems,' says Geoff Leesley. 'He has found it difficult to adjust to retire-ment. Not only is his health bad but he can't handle the tedium of having to plan meals each day — the sort of thing that women are always expected to do, whether they work or not, but which few men have much experience of. The Harrisons have moved up from Stamford in Lincolnshire and he's also found it hard to adapt geo-graphically. After all, Liverpool is totally different to Stamford. And his situation hasn't been helped by a certain lack of appreciation from Barbara. He has had to follow her up north but her life has hardly changed — she's still teaching, just at a different school.

'When the Harrisons got a brick through their conservatory window, John started up a homewatch scheme which Ron Dixon and Frank Rogers quickly turned into a vigi-lante group. Then he started steal-ing things. His kleptomania was just a symbol of his frustration with

The Close's most recent arrivals Barbara and John Harrison.

life. He's a reasonable chap but I think it all got too much for him.'

Manchester-born Geoff trained at RADA and has appeared in countless Shakespearean productions all over the country, including *Macbeth* and *Twelfth Night* at Birmingham, and *The Merchant of Venice* at Coventry. He also worked for the National Theatre in *The Provok'd Wife*, and played Malcolm in *Bedroom Farce* at London's Prince of Wales Theatre. Among his television credits are three prestigious Plays for Today — *Who's Our Little Jenny Lind?*, *The Amazing Miss Stella Estelle*, and *Another Flip For Dominic*. He has also enjoyed running parts in *Bergerac* (as DC Terry Wilson) and in four series of *Casualty* as ambulance-man Keith Cotterill.

'My main task on *Casualty* was to drive the ambulance,' says Geoff. 'I used to take my dog Lurch on set and he was always far more popular than me. The Producer used to say that if Lurch could have driven, he'd have got the part instead!'

Now 43, Geoff has been married to actress Bobbie Brown for 11 years. They live in Sussex and have two children.

Geoff concludes: 'Obviously I've tried to draw on my own experiences for John but to be honest I don't think we're that much alike. He goes in for all manner of competitions whereas I don't even do the Pools. And as for cooking, I leave it all to Bobbie because she's so good. Come to think of it, just about the only thing John and I have in common is that we've both got beards!'

NOVEMBER

Having been made redundant, Paul Collins moves into Brookside Close only to discover that his toilet has been stolen. Even though he has nothing to go on, he accuses his new neighbour, young Damon Grant. Middle-class Lucy Collins experiences intimidation on joining the local comprehensive school, while union leader Bobby Grant also feels intimidated by the attitude of the management at Fairbanks Engineering. A strike could be imminent. After Karen Grant has to fight off the attentions of her boyfriend Demon Duane, Barry seeks revenge on his sister's behalf. Paul Collins returns from the humiliation of signing-on to find that the entire Close has been burgled.

DECEMBER

Roger Huntington informs the City Planning Officer about the mounting pile of cookers in Gavin Taylor's garden. Gavin retaliates by erecting a multi-coloured shed made out of old doors. Bobby Grant is being blamed for the strike action so close to Christmas as it becomes clear that 200 workers will lose their jobs. Because of a bad school report, Damon misses out on a Christmas present, while Barry's present is a knife wound in the side from a mystery assailant. At the Law Society Dinner, Roger Huntington sees one of the senior partners at his law firm make a pass at his wife Heather. The Grants throw a party and they all conga out into the Close to welcome the New Year.

Gavin Taylor (Daniel Webb) says it with flowers to Barry Grant (Paul Usher).

THE STORY SO FAR
1983

JANUARY

Petra Taylor is desperate for a baby and a visit to the doctor leads Gavin to feel that the finger is being pointed at him for their fertility problems. Paul Collins confidently goes for a job interview but is subsequently rejected, so wife Annabelle sets out to supplement the family income by doing some supply teaching. Barry comes face to face with his attacker, Duane, but the police intervene in the nick of time. Barry 'scores' with Irene Harrison, the sex-starved wife of his football team manager, while Sheila discovers a card of contraceptive pills in Barry's bedroom. Barry gives a weak excuse about the Pill but Sheila won't swallow it — she thinks the card belongs to Karen.

FEBRUARY

Petra Taylor goes upstairs to find Gavin dead in bed. He had suffered a brain haemorrhage. When Matty Nolan learns that he is to be one of the 200 redundancies at Fairbanks, he falls out with his pal Bobby Grant. Barry doesn't want to continue seeing Irene Harrison and goes out with new girlfriend Carol instead. The irate Irene turns up and creates a scene. Carol storms off, vowing never to see Barry again. Karen receives a Valentine's card from Damon's mate Gizzmo and Heather does her best to cool the passion of Roger's boss Derek Hobbs. But Hobbs indicates that Roger's career could depend on her co-operation.

MARCH

Barry wastes no time in planning to ask out the widowed Petra but she nips his ardour in the bud by revealing that she thinks she is pregnant. The Huntingtons are burgled again and the Educational Welfare Officer calls at the Grants to discuss Damon's absenteeism from school. Sheila is made redundant and, to fill her time, is roped into joining Annabelle Collins' newly-formed Ratepayers' Association. Lucy Collins is spurned by boyfriend Jonathan and arranges for brother Gordon to spend Easter with his friend Mark Gossage.

APRIL

Against all the odds, Barry and Petra are going out on a regular basis — even in the face of wagging tongues implying that Barry could be the father of Petra's baby. Eccentric computer programmer Alan Partridge moves into the bungalow, number 6, and Damon and

DEATHS

FEBRUARY

Gavin Taylor

his mates Ducksie and Gizzmo, who had been using the unoccupied building as a secret den of vice, listen to his tales about his companion Sam. They reckon he is gay. But Sam turns out to be ex-model Samantha. Karen Grant outrages Mum Sheila by telling her she's not going to church anymore and Barry and his pal Terry Sullivan are caught stealing materials from Barry's work. Barry gets the sack.

MAY

Alan asks Samantha to marry him. She says no but decides to move in. Heather and Roger have another of their silly squabbles. She refuses to pick him up that evening from work and then, on his way home, he is run over and ends up in hospital with four broken ribs. Paul Collins turns down the offer of a job because it is below his abilities and rows over Lucy's involvement with CND. Bobby takes Sheila to London for the F.A. Cup Final weekend but returns home to hear disturbing news from the union's George Williams about the likely closure of the factory.

JUNE

Barry and Petra sneak off to the Isle of Man for the TT Races but on the boat trip back, Petra starts to feel unwell and suffers a miscarriage. Barry doesn't even bother to visit her in hospital. Paul Collins arrives for an interview at the Dole Office since his year of unemployment is up. It is suggested to him that he become a YOP's organiser. Lucy skips her French 'O' Level exam in favour of picketing a council meeting on behalf of CND. She is led away by the police for causing a disturbance but escapes with a caution.

Annabelle is in a state about the whole business but Paul manages to calm the situation.

JULY

Sheila is distressed when Teresa Nolan turns up and asks if Bobby could give Matty a loan. Roger storms out in a rage over Heather's impulsive spending — it transpires that his irrational behaviour is the result of his attraction to a rich, attractive client, Diane McAllister. Barry tells Petra that he has no intention of doing her decorating. They argue and Barry marches off, reminding Petra of her final argument with Gavin. Even Terry gets angry with Barry when he refuses to commit himself over their business partnership. With Bobby's redundancy on the cards, Sheila settles for new seat covers instead of a new sofa and urges Bobby to fight the impending factory closure.

AUGUST

Irritated by Petra's continuing depression and by the demands of his family, Barry takes the money Sheila has collected for a kidney fund and heads for London. The strain on Petra builds up to the point where she can't even cope with going to the supermarket. She packs a case and leaves home, to the consternation of her sisters Marie and Michelle. Petra's car is found and a Detective starts asking questions about a recent attack on Samantha. Alan proposes to Sam again and they agree to have a competition to see who can earn the most money over the next three months. If Alan wins, Sam will get engaged. Lucy announces that she wants to go to France and Heather tries to track down the errant Roger.

1983

SEPTEMBER

Roger tells Heather that he has to go out on business as an excuse to spend more time with Diane. While she is tidying the house, Heather finds a tie pin in Roger's jacket and demands to know who gave it to him. He avoids the issue by going rugby training with Alan Partridge. Heather later accuses Roger of having an affair. He denies it but when Heather catches him on the phone to Diane, that is the last straw. It's Roger and out. Roger arrives at Diane's flat but she tells him that she's off to Barbados the next day. Roger is left out in the cold. Marie Jackson moves into her sister Petra's house with fireman husband George and sons Gary and Little George as a temporary measure while their house is being refurbished. And Bobby and Sheila celebrate their 25th Wedding Anniversary.

OCTOBER

A not-so-jolly Roger returns to the Close. Heather has gone to Belfast, so Annabelle gives him a key. He puts some bread under the grill and falls asleep but luckily the Jacksons smell the burning from next door and put the fire out before there is too much damage. In Belfast, Heather chats to an old friend, Will Thurley, and decides to make a go of life in England on her own. As far as she is concerned, she and Roger are finished. Following a Bring and Buy Sale to save Fairbanks, Sheila is invited to appear on a TV programme to talk about the fight to prevent the factory shutting down.

NOVEMBER

Retired railwayman Harry Cross moves into 7 Brookside Close with his wife Edna who succeeds in insulting the removal men. They dump her things on the pavement and leave. Harry's garden gnomes prove irresistible to the Jackson boys and on returning from the shops, Edna is amazed to see that they have 'walked' into Heather's garden. They later move round to the Grants and Marie is forced to defend her lads' reputations. She further antagonises Harry by calling his gnomes 'dwarves'. Fairbanks closes down and Bobby is left feeling emasculated by his unemployment. Alan loses a floppy disc and Barry decides to set fire to his Jaguar and claim the insurance. He and Terry drive to the beach but there isn't enough petrol left to burn the car. They leave the car to fetch a can but when they get back, they see the motor slowly sinking into the sands. Unwittingly, they have found a perfect way of disposing of the car — and one for which they are totally blameless.

DECEMBER

Marie makes another desperate effort to trace Petra by placing an advert in a newspaper. She stuns George and Michelle by announcing that she is going to set a place at Christmas dinner for Petra but then out of the blue the girls receive a Christmas card from their missing sister. Bobby and Matty are delivering festive hampers while Barry and Terry are trying to make a bob or two by selling perfume. They end up at a pub where they hear that there has been a warning on the radio about the very perfume they are selling. They make an on-the-spot business decision and clean the pub with the perfume in exchange for drinks.

THE STORY SO FAR
1984

JANUARY

Sheila Grant sets up a non-registered employment agency and tells Bobby and Barry that she expects their support. Sheila then has a blazing row with Marie about Barry's slovenly behaviour, Sheila as ever backing her wayward son to the hilt. Having lost his wager, Alan Partridge is over the proverbial moon when Sam asks him to marry her. On the big day, Alan's best man lets him down and he is forced to accept Paul Collins' offer to stand in. Sam is late arriving at the register office but worse is to follow. Just as she is about to 'pledge her troth', she has a change of heart and runs out of the service. Later she tells Alan that she loves him but can't marry him at the moment. It's goodbye Sam, goodbye Samantha. And after a bad dream, Marie receives a visit from the police — Petra has committed suicide at a guest house in Llandudno.

FEBRUARY

Marie Jackson still hasn't forgiven Barry. To her, he is public enemy number one. She believes that his reckless action in taking Petra to the Isle of Man caused the miscarriage that, in turn, led to her depression and suicide. Harry Cross, still puzzled by the betting slip that he has found in Edna's handbag, is horrified to learn that his son Kevin is living with a married woman and her child. Damon, thrown out of class at school, plays a trick on the teacher by spreading clingfilm on the staff room toilets. He gets the cane for his pains. While the lonely Alan Partridge seems to be setting his sights on Heather, Barry and Terry enter into a car valeting partnership.

MARCH

Harry tries a spot of mischievous matchmaking between Alan and Heather by inviting them both to tea. Anxious Alan asks Sheila to explain to a relieved Heather that he has no plans to get involved with her. Karen Grant plans to boycott meat in school dinners and Marie is shocked by the sudden appearance of her long-lost father Davey who claims that since Petra left no will, he is the next of kin and therefore it is his house. He tries to throw them out of the house until Heather turns up and tells them about Petra's will. And Annabelle Collins works as election agent for her friend, Independent candidate Robin Tate.

APRIL

Barry and Terry become involved in some dodgy video dealing with local villain Tommy McArdle. Matty Nolan is discovered by the DHSS to be doing illicit work through Sheila's agency. Sheila is distraught but her guilt turns to anger when Bobby returns home to find her arranging an agency job with Bob Cummings. Bobby orders him out of the house, which makes Sheila all the more determined to carry on with the agency. Alan Partridge is accused of plagiarism after trying to sell Gordon Collins' computer programme on his behalf. Alan reacts badly, gets drunk and lurches out into the Close, screaming abuse at the neighbours.

MAY

Bobby uncovers the truth about Barry's illegal activities and throws him out of the house but the two are soon reconciled...at least for the time being. Harry Cross suffers a severe attack of angina and, with his bed

THE STORY SO FAR
1984

moved downstairs, has to lower his sights to continue snooping on the Close. The relationship between Terry and Michelle continues to blossom but Gordon Collins suspects that his father Paul is up to no good with Dorothy Tate, still grieving after husband Robin walked out on her.

JUNE

Bobby and Sheila Grant relax in Spain for a couple of weeks. Sheila is hoping that away from the constrictions of Brookside Close, she will be able to pluck up enough courage to tell Bobby she is pregnant. To her relief and surprise, he is delighted by the shock news. Damon plans to make the most of his parents' absence with his new girlfriend Linda but his plans are constantly thwarted. Marie Jackson tries to get the twins a place at a private school but George is more interested in educating himself as he prepares to enter a pub quiz at The Swan. And Paul Collins starts his new job as Production Manager for a local chemical firm — but not before wife Annabelle has been spying on him.

JULY

Acting on a tip-off from Gordon, Alan Partridge is re-united with Samantha at the International Garden Festival. Once again, they plan to marry and Alan puts the bungalow on the market, having been offered a job in Kuwait. Harry and Edna Cross, after meeting up with their old friends Ralph and Grace Hardwick at the Garden Festival, have set their hopes on buying Alan's bungalow. On the day of his court case with the DHSS, Matty looks for support from Bobby. But, to his anger, none is forthcom-

ing. With everyone celebrating the fact that Alan and Sam have finally got married, Sheila is knocked down by a motorbike ridden by Karen's latest boyfriend Andrew. Sheila is not too badly injured but the doctor warns Bobby that there could be a risk to the unborn baby.

AUGUST

Michelle puts £2,000 into a tool-hire partnership with Barry and Terry but, to her amazement, Terry has another partnership in mind when he proposes marriage. Michelle and Terry decide to live together instead but Terry's anticipation is interrupted when Victor, one of Tommy McArdle's henchmen and an old acquaintance of Barry's, bursts in demanding an alibi for that afternoon. A warehouse has been broken into and thousands of pounds of cigarettes and spirits have been stolen. George Jackson, who had put out a fire at the warehouse, had drawn a plan of the place for Victor in The Swan, blissfully unaware of Victor's criminal designs. George is arrested and Annabelle Collins stands bail for him, much to Paul's

WEDDINGS

JULY

Alan & Samantha Partridge

George Jackson (Cliff Howells) awaits sentence.

annoyance. Terry is anxious to protect George but Barry is anxious to protect himself and doesn't tell George about Victor needing an alibi.

SEPTEMBER

George is beaten up by Tommy McArdle after asking for help. McArdle later tells George not to make a fuss if he gets sent down — he'll look after George's family. George pleads not guilty in court and to escape from the troubles, he and Marie spend a day out at a leisure park. George rescues a young boy from drowning. He is a hero for a moment — but only until he has to sign on at the police station. Meanwhile Harry and Edna move into the bungalow and plan to let number 7 to suitable tenants. Harry likes the look of two young nurses, Kate Moses and Sandra Maghie, particularly if they can cure his back pains. They tell him they'll be a third tenant, Pat Hancock. Harry can hardly wait to meet the girl.

OCTOBER

Harry puts on his familiar dried-prune face when he finally meets Pat. For Pat is no girl but a muscular hospital porter. Harry, whose morals are so strict that he makes Mary Whitehouse look like a loose woman, proceeds to spy on the trio at every opportunity. Arriving home in his new company car, Paul Collins is also put out by Pat — he considers that the old ambulance that Pat drives is lowering the tone of the Close. George's court case is not going well and Barry and Terry at last realise that they must help him. They try to do a deal with the police implicating McArdle. But

George is still found guilty and sentenced to 18 months imprisonment. Barry and Terry know they must face the consequences...and the fury of McArdle.

NOVEMBER

Barry and Terry are beaten up by McArdle. Terry is in intensive care. Barry decides that the future is bleak. He will leave home to make a fresh start in life. Ralph Hardwick's wife Grace dies, shortly after Harry and Edna had returned from a holiday with the couple. Ralph accepts Edna's offer to come and stay with the Crosses for a while and immediately starts decorating the living-room. He also suggests that Edna open a credit account at the bookies. And Harry finds himself conducting a deep and meaningful conversation with a dressed skeleton, the property of prankster Pat.

DECEMBER

It's odds-on that Edna's gambling addiction will end in disaster. She receives a letter threatening legal action unless she pays her debt and, in an effort to raise some cash, pawns her engagement and wedding rings. Marie decides to do something positive to get George out of prison and launches the Free George Jackson Campaign. Annabelle's career in catering is marred by an exploding casserole and Sandra is also in a stew — her husband, who is still living in Glasgow, has met another woman and wants a divorce. The heavily-pregnant Sheila plays a Christmas trick on Bobby by pretending that she has gone into labour, while Harry thinks he is having a heart attack. But it turns out to be a pin prick from a new shirt he has been given.

DEATHS

NOVEMBER

Grace Hardwick

THE STORY SO FAR
1985

JANUARY

In his new union capacity, Bobby Grant has a meeting with Paul Collins to discuss a maintenance contract at the factory. Paul assures him there will be no redundancies. They are interrupted by a phone call. Bobby dashes home in time to see Sheila give birth to baby Claire. But Paul is accused of taking a bribe of a year's free food in return for awarding the maintenance contract. Sandra's husband Ian turns up, demanding that she agree to a divorce. She refuses and he hits her. Pat throws him out of the house but Ian threatens to sue for divorce, citing Pat as co-respondent.

FEBRUARY

Tommy McArdle warns Marie to stop the campaign to free George. Little George is accidentally shot in the eye by a stray air gun pellet while playing in the woods. George absconds from prison but, after phoning Marie to ask about his son's condition, he is recaptured. Terry and Michelle move in with Marie and Terry starts up the car valet service again. At the Grants, Damon sets himself up selling bin bags with a mate, Neil Wilson, and encounters a certain Mrs Bancroft who leads Damon to believe that it's not just bin bags she desires. Sheila is depressed after the birth of Claire and is shocked when Bobby suggests having a vasectomy.

MARCH

Heather is working on a new account for Curzon Communications and meets the handsome Tom Curzon, the company Chairman. A stranger throws a brick through Marie's window. Reluctantly she decides to give up the campaign and

contemplates moving to Leeds to be nearer to George's prison. Sheila is furious with Bobby for conducting union meetings at home. Gordon Collins suddenly leaves home — and flees to France. Annabelle is visited by Mrs Duncan, the mother of one of Gordon's school friends, who suspects her son Christopher of having had a homosexual relationship with Gordon.

APRIL

After being dropped from the Curzon review for refusing to go out with Curzon Communications' Chief Accountant, Deaken Mathews, Heather suddenly finds herself back on the case. Tom Curzon sacks Mathews, asks Heather out and promptly invites her to spend a weekend in Portugal. Pat Hancock sets up a singing telegram service and persuades Damon to be a gorillagram at a children's party. Pat goes ape when Sandra is attacked by radiographer Jimmy Powell. Pat lashes out in revenge but breaks some equipment in the process and

Happier times. Heather (Amanda Burton) enjoys a business break in Portugal with Tom Curzon (Brian Stephens).

BIRTHS

JANUARY

Claire Grant

THE STORY SO FAR
1985

Neighbours. Everybody loves good neighbours. Billy Corkhill and Terry Sullivan argue over whose turn it is to mow the lawn.

DEATHS

AUGUST

Kate Moses

John Clarke

is suspended. Damon finds more reliable work as a painter and decorator on a YTS scheme. Claire Grant is christened, Karen and her boyfriend Andrew finally split up, and a strike at the factory divides Paul and Bobby. Marie Jackson leaves the Close.

MAY

Harry makes a complaint against bookmaker's Tattersall's, an outfit run by Tommy McArdle. Harry is offered £4,000 to drop his action. Edna is mugged on the way back from the Post Office after collecting her pension. Pat is sacked and learns that his ambulance, which had been stolen, has been written off. Relations between Terry and Michelle worsen as Terry accuses her of having an affair with her dancing teacher Richard de Saville. Terry gets a job at Tommy McArdle's club. Redundancy notices have been issued at the factory, leading to a doorstep showdown between Paul and Bobby.

JUNE

Tommy McArdle has been arrested and Terry is suspected of being the informant. After finding out that Michelle has been sleeping with Richard, a furious Terry destroys their bed. Michelle leaves the Close to join Marie in Leeds. Bobby is keen to end the strike and his manhood — he secretly makes an appointment to have a vasectomy. He returns home feeling sore and groggy. Sheila is disgusted when she eventually gets the truth out of him and moves into Claire's room. Window cleaner Sinbad starts to build a bonfire with rubbish collected from the residents, including Terry and Michelle's double bed. But the blaze flares out of control and the Fire Brigade are called out.

JULY

Sheila overhears Damon and Karen discussing her wilting relationship with Bobby. Kate recruits Sandra in her campaign to promote a 'halfway' house for mental patients to be built near the Close. When Harry hears about the proposal, he is predictably hostile. A distraught John Clarke arrives at the nurses' house and blames the hospital for his mother's death. He later returns, unbalanced and dangerous, and pulls a gun on the trio. They are held hostage and Pat begins to crack under the pressure. Annabelle Collins suspects something is amiss and calls the police. The Close is evacuated.

AUGUST

At a boarding house, the residents watch the siege on television. Kate persuades Clarke to release Pat and Sandra. Three shots are heard. The siege of *Brookside* is over — Kate and Clarke are dead. Pat blames

himself for her death. The Collins' holiday plans are scuppered when the travel company folds. They go camping instead. Damon takes photos of Karen and Claire for a Mother and Baby competition in the Gazette. They win. While Harry is out, Edna Cross collapses and a chip pan ignites. Terry saves the day but can do little to help Edna who has suffered a stroke and is unable to speak. Harry is mortified as she fails to respond to treatment but Ralph tells him he must keep going for Edna's sake.

SEPTEMBER
Pat and Sandra return from a romantic sojourn in Glasgow to find Harry in their house but their anger turns to pity when they hear that Edna has died. Terry moves in with Sandra and Pat but is unable to bring all his property because Pat fails to turn up with the van. The Corkhills move into the Jacksons' old house. Their first act is to dump Terry's belongings out on the lawn. Pat and Terry set up a van hire business. Meanwhile, young Rod Corkhill is infatuated with Heather and Tracy Corkhill persuades Dad Billy to let her go on a school skiing holiday, even though they can't really afford it.

OCTOBER
Karen Grant goes to university. It soon transpires that Billy Corkhill has handled more stolen goods than Shaw Taylor and he supplies Annabelle with a burglar alarm, which, if not bent, is decidedly curved. Tom Curzon asks Heather to be 'Mrs. Curzon' for the evening so that he can impress some clients but Heather refuses. He responds by asking her to marry him and, follow-

ing consultations with her mother, she accepts. They plan the wedding but Tom refuses to invite his daughter Rowena and dashes off to America on company business.

NOVEMBER
Julia Brogan, Doreen Corkhill's mother, is heavily fined for fiddling her electricity meter. Lucy Collins, back from France, is seeing a married man, James Fleming, while Tracy Corkhill also has a mystery boyfriend, about whom she seems to feel particularly guilty. There is a hitch in the wedding preparations as Tom and Heather argue about his deception in keeping the existence of his daughter secret from his father Jim. Heather realises that she cannot marry Tom after all and calls off the wedding. Driving through the city on business, she bumps into an MG Midget driven by architect Nicholas Black.

DECEMBER
At work decorating a smart house, Damon sees a colleague stealing a vase. He is persuaded to keep quiet about it but is then wrongly accused of stealing the ornament himself and is suspended. Damon still refuses to clear his name but Sheila confronts the real thief, threatening to reveal the truth unless the vase is returned. Damon is duly asked to go back to work. Pat and Terry meet a formidable but attractive rival in the van hire business, Vicki Cleary, and Karen goes on a date with Guy Willis. Billy Corkhill crosses a picket line at his factory, bringing him into conflict with Bobby who is there to support his union men. Sinbad turns up with a bargain Christmas turkey for Sheila. It's so fresh that it's still alive.

DEATHS

SEPTEMBER

Edna Cross

99

JANUARY

Barry's ex-girlfriend Jane is staying at Sandra and Pat's. She is a heroin addict. They are worried about her influence on the Close's youngsters but before they have the chance to throw her out, she runs off with their valuables. Nick Black calls on Heather because he has heard nothing about the insurance claim for the damage to his car. He offers to help her decorate and asks her out for a meal. Lucy's friend James, who is also her boss, comes for dinner. Later, when Paul and Annabelle say that they suspect he is married, they are horrified when Lucy calmly announces that she knows he is. She refuses to give him up and tells them to stop interfering. Pat and Barry become involved in a van war with the Clearys, while Rod Corkhill is suspended from school for attacking a teacher, Peter Montague, after seeing graffiti about sister Tracy. It proclaimed, 'Tracy Corkhill gave Monty a Swiss roll.'

FEBRUARY

Julia says that she saw a love letter from Tracy to someone called Peter and eventually Tracy reveals that she has been having an affair with Peter Montague, the teacher who took them to Switzerland. Billy tries to think things over calmly and rationally so he goes to school and thumps Montague. The police arrest Billy, and Tracy briefly runs away from home. Billy decides to keep quiet about Tracy's affair with Montague for fear of dragging his daughter's name through the mud. James tries to end his fling with Lucy but she angrily confronts his wife. James tells Lucy to go and she loses her job as well as her man. Heather meets Nick's ex-wife

Barbara and realises she is a lesbian. And Harry puts an advert in the personal columns.

MARCH

Harry and Ralph go through the replies to Harry's advert and both agree that Madge Richmond sounds the ideal candidate. Harry mucks up the meeting but Ralph and Madge get along famously. Billy is sentenced to three months in prison but Doreen reveals the reason he hit Montague. He is released on bail, pending an appeal. Pat and Sandra grow apart but Terry and Vicki Cleary grow closer. Sheila has been on a further education course but Bobby is jealous of her tutor Alun Jones. Sheila is racked with guilt about not telling her friend Teresa that husband Matty is having an affair. Karen finally agrees to spend the night with Guy but is unable to have sex.

APRIL

Having agreed to go on holiday to Torquay with Ralph, Madge is none too pleased to discover that Harry has decided to tag along, too. Ralph promises to find Harry a companion. Harry thinks it's going to be Heather but instead it's Julia Brogan! Damon also goes to Torquay, in search of a job. Bobby and Sheila accuse each other of being wrapped up in their own little worlds — his with the union, hers with her course. Sheila receives an anonymous threatening letter and wonders if Matty sent it, trying to warn her off. She also receives sinister phone calls. Nick tries to defend Heather in front of her odious boss Keith Tench while Paul and Annabelle are horrified when, having at last got over James, Lucy announces that she is off to France again to sell videos with, of all people, Barry Grant. Billy Corkhill wins his appeal but loses his job.

MAY

Paul's firm is taken over and he is made redundant. Heather accepts Nick's offer of marriage. With Billy out of work, the bills are piling up, the grounded Tracy having resorted to Chatline. And to make matters worse, Billy's errant brother Jimmy turns up with a pile of 'hot' bricks to build a garage. Madge teaches Harry to drive. Karen is relaxed after losing her virginity to Guy but Heather is on edge about meeting Nick's children. And when Nick's son Adam is knocked down by a car while walking home from a cricket match, the other two, Ruth and Scott, blame Heather.

JUNE

Law and order finally come to *Brookside*. Rod Corkhill announces that he wants to join the police and Annabelle Collins is applying to be a magistrate. However she worries that Paul's involvement in a road safety blockade will jeopardise her chances. Pat is bitterly jealous over Sandra's involvement with Dr. Tony Hurrell on a case of professional malpractice and becomes increasingly violent. Matty says he is leaving Teresa for Mo. Sheila accosts Mo, who admits sending the threatening letter. But Sheila's powers of persuasion get through to the other woman and Mo tells Matty she wants their relationship to end. Just starting out are Heather and Nick, celebrating their wedding day.

JULY

Trouble is looming for Sheila Grant.

First she discovers the identity of the anonymous phone caller. It is Ken Dinsdale, whose wife Sally had come to Sheila for help after being beaten up by him. Then Matty accuses Sheila of turning Mo against him and has to be thrown out of the house by Damon, back from Torquay. And Alun Jones is becoming dangerously obsessed with her. On her way back from a pub meeting with Jones, Sheila gets into a taxi but is pursued by Matty, who accuses her of hypocritically having an affair with the tutor. Sheila gets out of the taxi to walk and is raped. The immediate police suspect is Pat, fresh from a blazing row with Sandra, which has left him with scratch-marks on his face. But when Pat's alibi is confirmed, Matty is arrested.

WEDDINGS

JUNE

Nicholas & Heather Black

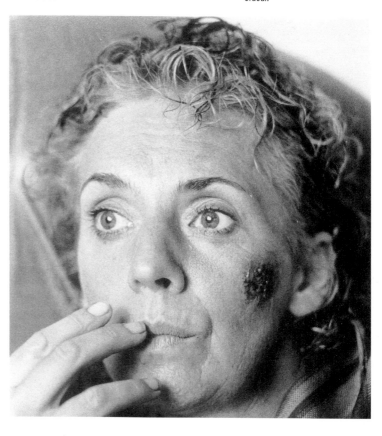

A haunted Sheila after her rape ordeal.

THE STORY SO FAR
1986

AUGUST

On hearing that a man has been charged, Teresa assumes it is Matty. But in fact he has been released and returns home to find a suicide note from Teresa. She drowns herself in the Mersey. The cab driver confesses to Sheila's rape. Paul is arrested at a road safety blockade and Nick agrees to let his shifty pal Charlie move into the flat, which he refuses to give up despite living with Heather. When Gordon returns home, Paul and Annabelle are delighted to see that he is with a girl Cecile. But their hopes are dashed when Cecile reveals that Gordon has been her brother Pierre's lover in France.

SEPTEMBER

Gordon's gay friend from school, Christopher Duncan, turns up. When the *Gay Times* is accidentally delivered to the Corkhills', Paul admits to an incredulous Billy that it is Gordon's. Pat falls prey to maneater Andrea and asks Sandra to move out. She refuses. Dr. Hurrell comes round to say goodbye, but instead he and Sandra end up in bed together. His bedside manner wins her round and they leave the Close for good. Tracy Corkhill takes up modelling, Damon meets a new girlfriend, Gail, and Karen moves in with Guy. Back from a trip to Hong Kong, Heather realises that Nick has a major secret and that Charlie is somehow involved. Nick's daughter Ruth finally reveals the truth — Nick and Charlie are heroin addicts.

OCTOBER

Nick vows to Heather that he will never take heroin again. But he is soon back on it, supplied by the omnipresent Charlie. Rod has his police interview, worrying all the time that probing questions might rake up secrets about the Corkhills' criminal past. Sheila is having nightmares about the rape but Barry believes he knows the best way to help her. He asks Tommy McArdle to have the rapist beaten up. McArdle agrees in return for a favour. The favour is a trip to Barbados for Pat and Terry.

NOVEMBER

Pat and Terry accompany Tommy McArdle's Mum to Barbados. They think she is senile but she leaves a mysterious parcel in the locker at the airport. Pat is more concerned with getting off with Avril, the courier, but Terry is suspicious of the whole business. And with good reason, too — as the old lady collects an envelope in Barbados, conceals it in a case and gets Terry to carry it home through customs. The Corkhills' financial worries are building up, with Billy out of work again and dozy Doreen spending money so fast she makes Viv Nicholson look thrifty. Meanwhile, Heather finally realises she can never get Nick off heroin and, acting on Barry's advice, asks him to leave.

DECEMBER

Death is in the Close. Harry Cross's granddaughter is born prematurely and dies. Harry blames himself for upsetting his daughter-in-law Sally. Nick takes a fatal overdose of heroin. Heather identifies the body and leaves on the boat for Ireland without saying she'll be back. Karen and Guy split up, as do Damon and the pushy Gail. Chez Corkhill, the phone and the electricty are cut off, the TV is re-possessed and Tracy starts a YTS hairdressing scheme.

THE STORY SO FAR
1987

JANUARY

Billy Corkhill gets a job in Tunbridge Wells but Tracy wants to pack in hairdressing. Mr. Rod the policeman goes off to Police College and promises to be faithful to his latest girlfriend Kirsty. Karen Grant has gone to London but Damon takes up with a new girl, Debbie. Harry is highly suspicious of Madge and tries to warn Ralph off her but Ralph and Madge head off on holiday to Spain. Bobby learns of an asbestos problem at Billinge Chemicals and is convinced there's a cover-up. Sheila plans a spiritual trip to Rome and, to Bobby's disgust, gets a part-time job at The Swan to pay for it.

FEBRUARY

Paul rescues a drowning puppy and christens it Lucky. Ralph and Madge return from holiday engaged. Harry rejects the presents they have bought him. Ralph is eagerly looking forward to the wedding but Harry has laid a trap by placing a lonely hearts ad. Among his replies is one from Madge. Harry meets Madge and accuses her of being a gold-digger. She confesses that she has other men in her life and agrees to call off the engagement. Even then, she explains it away by inventing some fabrication about grief for her late husband.

MARCH

The unsuspecting Ralph accuses Harry of being spiteful and jealous and leaves, only to return on learning the truth about Madge from Julia. Pat finds himself a nice little earner acting as road manager for an all-girl band. Gordon and Chris live out a fantasy and rush out of a restaurant without paying.

Returning to the Close in a stolen car, they kill Lucky. An anguished Paul is convinced that Pat killed the dog and, despite Gordon's pleading, takes revenge by reporting Pat and Terry to the DHSS. When Pat confronts Paul, Gordon admits that he was responsible for Lucky's death. Pat puts up a banner on the front of the Collins' house telling the world that Paul is a DHSS spy. After a visit from Doreen, Billy comes back from Tunbridge Wells and Tracy is sacked by her hairdressing boss Shelley for being rude.

APRIL

Young solicitors Jonathan Gordon-Davies and Laura Wright arrive at 9 Brookside Close and start decorating. Laura looks forward to moving in, but not to all the fuss and expense of the wedding. Bobby reluctantly agrees to accompany Sheila to Rome. Tracy gets her job back and Jimmy suggests a fake burglary as a way of paying off all the Corkhills' debts. Jimmy duly burgles the house and Billy makes

Rod Corkhill (Jason Hope) prepares to iron out his differences with Kirsty (Joanne Black).

out a false insurance claim. Paul and Annabelle come home from collecting Annabelle's mother, Mona, to find they have been burgled. It is the handiwork of Jimmy, in an attempt to make the crime at the Corkhills' appear authentic. Harry informs Pat and Terry of his plans to sell number 7.

MAY

Mona lives up to her name — she is convinced that Paul is trying to poison her. Vicki agrees to move in with Terry but only on condition that he gets rid of Pat, from both the house and the business. When Terry teeters, Vicki vanishes. Debbie's father goes to the Grants to tell Damon not to see his daughter anymore. The road to marriage is far from smooth for Jonathan and Laura, particularly when they drive into a large hole that has suddenly appeared in the Close. Mona writes to her son Teddy on the Wirral to complain about Paul but, as she goes to post the letter, she too falls victim to the black hole.

JUNE

Repossession proceedings start against the Corkhills. Doreen's dentist boss Howman offers to lend her money but wants re-paying in kind. She can't go through with it and packs in her job. She shows Billy the repossession letter and Billy vents his anger by driving recklessly over the neighbours' lawns. Billy decides to resort to crime and asks Jimmy to explore his underworld contacts. Laura postpones the wedding because of an important case. Harry and Ralph receive betting tips from beyond the grave when a medium seems to contact Edna — but alas, they back the wrong horse.

JULY

Christopher upsets Gordon by letting out Mona's house in Kendal to Ralph for a holiday. Gordon demands the rent money. Debbie's father, Mr. McGrath, fixes up Damon with a job in Ipswich but Damon assures him that it won't have the desired effect — he is still intent on seeing Debbie. Tracy steals a key to the hairdresser's where she works and she and her boyfriend Jamie use the sunbed there. There ain't no sunshine with Harry Cross who tries to buy out Terry and Pat and offers them £100 to leave. They reject it but Pat implies that he would go if Harry increased the sum.

AUGUST

Bobby gets his first AIDS case at work. The victim, Stan McHugh, wants to keep his job but doubts Bobby's determination to help him do so. To prove his sincerity, Bobby invites Stan to tea and eventually plucks up the courage to tell Sheila what he's done. Local villain Gene offers Billy a 'job' as getaway driver on a supermarket raid. At the reception following Jonathan and Laura's wedding, Billy chats to guests to establish his alibi. Then he sneaks out to join the rest of the gang. The robbery goes wrong and the supermarket manager is stabbed. Billy drives him to hospital and dumps him. Billy is terrified that the manager will identify him. The rest of the gang don't want Billy grassing on them and, to underline the point, they mug Tracy. Tracy knows something is wrong when she later spots Billy with her attacker.

SEPTEMBER

Harry pays Pat £500 to leave and

WEDDINGS

AUGUST

Jonathan & Laura Gordon-Davies

THE STORY SO FAR
1987

Mona goes on the rampage with a trowel. Billy confesses about the robbery to Doreen. Rod, oblivious to his father's involvement, proudly announces that the police have picked up the rest of the gang — it's only the driver who's still on the loose. In keeping with the mood in the Corkhills' house, Tracy and Jamie paint her bedroom black. Billy, incriminated by Gene, is taken in for questioning and an identity parade is held. He fears the worst but amazingly, the supermarket manager Riordan doesn't pick him out. Billy is mystified.

OCTOBER
Tracy hides Jamie, who has been kicked out of his home, in the Corkhills' garage. They come to the conclusion that Billy was involved in the attempted robbery. Just as Billy thinks he has got away with it, Riordan attempts to blackmail him into robbing his supermarket for him. Jonathan is annoyed to arrive home and find Laura's perfectionist father Geoff in the house — he has come to repair a cracked light switch on the landing. Later, alone in the house, Laura switches on the light and receives a mighty electric shock which sends her crashing down the stairs. Damon and Debbie leave home. Sheila thinks that she and Bobby have let them down.

NOVEMBER
Laura lies unconscious in hospital. Barry gets a nasty shock when he learns that his latest girlfriend Ursula is also romantically involved with ruthless stuttering villain Sizzler. Doreen vows to leave Billy if he has anything to do with Riordan. Billy succumbs to the blackmail threat and Doreen walks out.

Riordan backs off when Billy calls his bluff but, in a note, Doreen insists that she has gone for good. Terry moves in with Jonathan who, getting a shock from the faulty landing light switch, realises that Geoff Wright's wiring caused Laura's accident. A policeman arrives at the Grants to tell them that Damon has been stabbed to death in York. Bobby unjustly blames Debbie for Damon's death.

DECEMBER
Chrissy and Frank Rogers turn up in an articulated lorry to rent number 7 from Harry. Working as Santa Claus in place of his father Jack who is ill, Terry chats up Jonathan's secretary Sue. Mona, who is in a home, comes to spend Christmas with Paul and Annabelle and insists that the people at the home are trying to kill her. Nobody pays any attention. The Wrights, unaware that Geoff's DIY skills caused Laura's fall, argue with Jonathan about his attitude towards Laura. They are convinced she will recover but he is more realistic and is prepared to agree to organ donation.

Sheila is inconsoleable at Damon's grave.

DEATHS

NOVEMBER

Damon Grant

THE STORY SO FAR
1988

JANUARY

Laura is declared brain dead. The doctors want to switch off the artificial ventilator. The Wrights come round to the idea of organ donation and, after the operation, their daughter is allowed to die. Jonathan realises that he will have to lie at the inquest to save Geoff from the awful truth. To get away from it all, he tries to persuade Terry to join him on a skiing holiday. Chrissy Rogers learns that her son 'Growler' has been skipping school and urges lorry-driver Frank to pursue the desk job that he has been promised. Bobby and Sheila Grant drift further apart.

FEBRUARY

Billy goes to Bristol in search of Doreen, while Sheila follows a boy thinking it's Damon. Paul confiscates Growler's football but the boys get their own back by hoisting a chair on to the roof of the Collinses' house. Chrissy Rogers rows with the school over daughter Sammy's new, non-regulation school coat. Gordon is immobilised after a motorbike accident, Bobby loses his licence after being caught drinking and driving, while Barry discovers that Debbie is pregnant and that her father wants her to have an abortion. Jamie, Jimmy and Jimmy's mistress Kathy all move into the Corkhills' home for waifs and strays. And Harry uncovers an obscure rule to defeat Ralph and so win the election for Entertainment and Concert Secretary at the Commonwealth and Empire Club.

MARCH

During Harry's inaugural speech, Councillor Redfearn dies and the Third Light Rule takes effect. This means the whole committee has to be re-elected! Ralph organises the entertainment for Commonwealth Day but inadvertently books a male stripper. Julia saves the day by singing and it is revealed that both Harry and Ralph have been elected to the committee. Perturbed by Mona's repeated claims that she is being physically maltreated at the home, Paul and Annabelle pay a visit. Matron explains away the injuries by saying that Mona has had an accident. Paul and Annabelle believe her but Gordon and Christopher go to the home unannounced to check things out. Their suspicions of ill-treatment are confirmed and they bring Mona back to Brookside. Terry hears that he has got his taxi licence. Jonathan and Terry go skiing in Austria and meet two Canadian girls, Cheryl and Donna.

APRIL

Rod and Jamie go to London in search of the missing Tracy, while Jimmy finishes off building an extension to the Corkhills'. Cheryl and Donna pay a surprise visit on Jonathan and Terry in Liverpool, to the irritation of Sue, who is jealous of the warm welcome Terry gives the girls and to the disgust of Geoff Wright, who thinks Jonathan has got a new girlfriend already. Geoff threatens to have another inquest into Laura's death. Frank Rogers is interrogated by the police about the theft of his lorry. The load eventually turns up and Frank, although charged with serious misconduct, hangs on to his job. While Bobby is obsessed with union business, Sheila sees a marriage guidance counsellor in a vain attempt to repair their own ailing union.

THE STORY SO FAR
1988

MAY

Sheila and Kathy go out to a club, leaving Bobby to return to an empty house. Furious, he throws a suitcase of Sheila's things on to the Close. He storms over to the Corkhills' and finds Billy babysitting Claire. Bobby smashes Billy's front door and when Sheila returns, Bobby slaps her face. Bobby leaves Sheila and the house is put up for sale. Sheila and Claire go to Basingstoke, Mona decides to go and stay with her beloved Teddy, and Annabelle goes on a magistrates' course to Shrewsbury. Harry's garden gnomes go missing.

JUNE

In Shrewsbury, Annabelle is drawn closer to one of her colleagues on the course, Brian Lawrence. Gordon and Christopher are charged after being involved in a fight with a gang of lads who followed them coming out of a club. Sizzler has a job for Barry — he's to get to know a woman called Penny. Barry's dubious charms soon work and he takes Penny to a designated hotel room, where they make love. Afterwards, Sizzler enters holding a video of their exploits. He uses it to blackmail Penny as a means of gaining control of her husband Franco's betting shops.

JULY

Sheila comes back from Basingstoke and Barry asks if there is any chance of a reconciliation with Bobby. Kathy is worried about where Sheila will live when the house is sold and persuades Billy to let Sheila stay at the Corkhills' if the need arises. Sheila visits Damon's grave and finds Karen at the cemetery too. They talk about the marital breakdown. Geoff 'Growler' Rogers briefly runs away from home after a model is stolen from school and his sister Sammy goes on an Animal Rights demonstration. Over at the Collinses' Mona returns unexpectedly from Teddy's.

AUGUST

The Collinses receive a series of threatening phone calls and Annabelle seems prepared to embark on an affair with Brian Lawrence. But first she and Paul take a nervous Mona to her new home. On their return, they discover the house covered in abusive anti-gay slogans. When the phone rings again, Paul provokes the callers and a blazing car is left outside his house. On a business trip to Canada, Jonathan seeks out Cheryl. They get on well and she calls off her proposed wedding to run away with him. Back at the Close, Sue and Terry declare their love for one another.

SEPTEMBER

Barry is forced to do another job for Sizzler who wants control of Ma Johnston's gaming arcade. Barry is to kill Ma's dog and deliver its head to her if she won't co-operate. After renting a squalid bedsit, Sheila finally accepts Billy's offer and she

Would you buy a used car off this man? Annabelle Collins (Doreen Sloane) obviously thought Brian Lawrence (Vincent Maguire) had passed his M.O.T.

THE STORY SO FAR
1988

and Claire move into the Corkhills' extension. Chrissy Rogers becomes increasingly worried about the standard of son Geoff's school work and decides to get his eyes tested. Cheryl comes to England and is accepted by the Manchester Business School. Sammy Rogers starts work at a supermarket while Tracy Corkhill gets a new hairdressing job where she has to cope with the unwelcome attentions of the manager Gerrard.

OCTOBER

Cheryl has moved in with Jonathan and contracts have been exchanged on the Grants' house. While cleaning windows, Jamie breaks the Collinses' sink and replaces their bathroom suite with the one from the Grants' empty house. But when Barry returns, he switches the water back on and floods the bathroom. The potential buyer is not amused. House problems too for the Rogers: they want to buy the home they are renting from Harry but old Crossy rejects their offer and issues them with a notice to quit. Unknowingly, he then accepts a lower offer from Chrissy, made anonymously. Gordon and Chris split up. Sheila catches Annabelle kissing Brian Lawrence.

NOVEMBER

Terry presents Sue with an engagement ring. Sue behaves strangely — all the more so when she encounters one of her old flames, Martin. She tries to convince a hurt Terry that it's him she wants and not Martin. At Annabelle's request, Brian Lawrence gives Gordon a job in his car showroom. When Annabelle's car goes in for a service, Gordon spots that the mechanics have scrawled 'the boss's bit on the side' into the dirt on it. He too sees his mother kissing Brian who then admits to Gordon that they are having an affair. Chrissy and Frank dress up as Arabs to buy the house off Harry. When Harry finds he has been tricked and that the mystery buyers are the Rogers, he goes into a major sulk.

DECEMBER

Tracy is sacked by her boss Gerrard. Sheila advises her to take him to an Industrial Tribunal. Paul finds out about Annabelle and Brian and confronts them about their affair. Brian gallantly leaves Annabelle to face the music. She, in turn, storms out. Paul is a broken man. Terry rescues Cheryl from a fire at Jonathan's, while Barry and Sinbad unwittingly sell poisonous cuddly seals, one of which kills Ralph's dog Rommel. Chrissy Rogers comes to the conclusion that son Geoff is dyslexic. At the Corkhills', Damon's girlfriend Debbie turns up out of the blue with Sheila's grandson Simon. Sheila is overjoyed and is getting closer to Billy. For his part, Billy says he no longer wants Doreen back. Sheila seeks guidance from a priest who reminds her that she is still married to Bobby. Sheila remains torn between her heart and head.

Jonathan Gordon - Davies has plenty on his mind, and Cheryl on his shoulder.

THE STORY SO FAR
1989

JANUARY

Gordon stitches up Brian Lawrence by selling his cars off cheaply. Harry proposes to his friend Betty but she turns him down. Cheryl urges Jonathan to exorcise the ghost of Laura by redecorating the house. Rod has had a fling with a pretty young policewoman, Emma, and has to try to explain away the scratch marks on his back to Kirsty. In an effort to prove his sincerity, he is coerced into proposing to Kirsty. Chrissy and Frank argue over Geoff's dyslexia. Frank doesn't want to seek private help but Chrissy is adamant that Geoff is not receiving sufficient assistance at school. Billy tells Sheila he loves her but when Barry discovers them in bed together, there is an almighty row.

FEBRUARY

Tracy finishes with Jamie and Mona reveals that she's getting married to Gerald Fallon, a fellow resident at the home where she is staying. After two months of sniping, Paul and Annabelle realise how much they love one another. Their reconciliation has begun. Chrissy obtains a private assessment which confirms Geoff to be dyslexic but when she presents Mr. Jenkins, the Pastoral Head at Geoff's school, with the report, she is told that it is not recognised by the Authority. She angrily removes her son from the school and decides to teach him herself at home. Sue discovers that she is pregnant — but can't bring herself to tell Terry that the baby is not his.

MARCH

Sue tells Cheryl that Martin is the father of the baby she is expecting. She contemplates abortion but is unable to go through with it. As she becomes increasingly irritable, Sue blurts out to Terry that she is pregnant. He is thrilled, thinking the baby is his. Jonathan and a colleague at work, Sarah, plan to set up their own legal firm. Owen Daniels woos Sammy Rogers but Chrissy finds that teaching Geoff at home is no easy matter. After he has locked himself in the bathroom, she concedes defeat and takes him back to school. Gerrard attempts to persuade Tracy to drop her tribunal case but, encouraged by Kirsty, she persists and wins £1,500 damages and costs. She also gets her job back.

APRIL

On her first day back at work, Tracy hears one of Gerrard's former customers insulting her and complaining about his sacking. Tracy reacts

WEDDINGS

APRIL

Gerald & Mona Fallon

Annabelle Collins' mother, Mona, weds Gerald Fallon.

THE STORY SO FAR
1989

by spraying the woman's face with hot water. She later offers to resign but her new boss, Antony, refuses to accept her notice. Mona marries Gerald. Frank Rogers goes to the auction of the Grants' old house and, seized by auction fever, buys it. Cheryl finds the pressure of living with Terry, Sue and Sue's secret — in the house Jonathan shared with Laura — too much to handle. She implores Jonathan to move.

MAY

Michael, Caroline and Jessica Choi arrive as the new residents of 7 Brookside Close. The Rogers' move into number 5. Chrissy's appeal for Geoff's educational needs results in him receiving specialist tuition from a peripatetic teacher. Frank is over the moon when Geoff is invited to be a trialist with Tranmere Rovers Football Club. A livid Kirsty finds out about Rod and Emma and promptly calls off the impending nuptials. Sheila starts work as a school dinner lady and is pleased to be able to help a deaf girl pupil. Sue finally agrees to marry Terry.

JUNE

Convinced that she is a poor second to Jonathan's work and that he has no intention of looking for a new home for them, Cheryl packs her bags and flies back to Canada. Sinbad falls in love with Caroline Choi but the feeling definitely isn't mutual. Michael Choi meets Alison Gregory and they are soon attracted to one another, once Alison has established that Michael and Caroline are brother and sister. Bitter over Cheryl's departure, Jonathan informs Sue that he knows it is Martin's baby and threatens to tell Terry. Spotting

that Cheryl's luggage is to go to Manchester, Jonathan tracks her down and pleads with her to give him another chance.

JULY

Jonathan finally buys a flat, having rented the old house to Terry and Sue, and persuades Cheryl to continue their relationship. Harry Cross is in a turmoil over the moving of Edna's grave. Annabelle Collins tries to help a young offender, Louise, who turns up on her doorstep. The comparative peace at the Corkhills' is shattered by the sudden return of Doreen. She discovers that Sheila and Billy are lovers. Sheila tells Billy he must throw Doreen out. When he fails to do so, Sheila walks out. Doreen is determined to win Billy back.

AUGUST

Sue and Terry get married. With the baby due, Terry decides he can't continue to work such long hours with the taxi and asks his friend Mick Johnson to take over his day shift. Ralph meets Lana Costello, an American friend of Gerald and Mona, Mick Johnson temporarily moves in with Harry, and Michael Choi's father is unhappy about the blossoming relationship with Alison. Sheila and Billy go to Ireland. Encouraged by Tracy, an indignant Doreen removes Sheila's and Claire's belongings from the house and has the front door lock changed. Doreen tells Tracy the truth about the supermarket robbery. On their return, Sheila, listening to Billy and Doreen arguing, also learns about Billy's criminal past. Sheila finishes with Billy and, after Billy tells Doreen he doesn't love her, Doreen leaves too.

WEDDING

AUGUST

Terry & Sue Sullivan

THE STORY SO FAR
1989

SEPTEMBER

Sheila and Billy are re-united. Sue gives birth to a baby boy. Cheryl is irked when Jonathan says he would like to be a father too. Louise tells Annabelle that someone has been touching her at home and it becomes apparent that that someone is Louise's brother, Gary. Scared of being left alone, that little charmer Harry warns Ralph off Lana and tells Lana that Ralph is just after her money. Harry's skullduggery is all in vain. Ralph asks Lana to marry him. She accepts and says they'll live in Las Vegas.

OCTOBER

Sammy Rogers, her friends Ronnie and Nisha, and her boyfriend Owen go on a night out with two lads Kav and Tony. Owen suspects the car the lads are driving is stolen and his fears are confirmed when the police give chase. The car crashes. The two lads are killed and Owen is left in a coma. Sammy is full of guilt. While Alison and her daughter Hattie move in with Michael Choi, Lana and Ralph leave the Close. In an emotional farewell, Harry buries the hatchet and makes a last-minute dash to the station to say goodbye.

NOVEMBER

Sammy turns to drink. Young Katie Rogers is being bullied at school by a girl called Bagga. Paul asks about fostering Louise but is shocked to find that she has been stealing money. Louise runs away and the Collinses have second thoughts. Sheila applies for a care assistant's job at the Deaf School and Billy lands a contract to wire up a wool shop. When the owner, Mr. Trevor, is slow paying up, Jimmy, clearly unhinged, takes the door off the shop. Trevor's sons retaliate by removing the doors from Billy's car so Jimmy runs amok with a fire extinguisher in the wool shop. A vendetta begins.

DECEMBER

Billy and Jimmy go to the wool shop to strip all the electrical fittings that Jimmy installed. The distressed Mr. Trevor collapses. The wool shop then sends a JCB to dig up Billy's front lawn. Eventually peace is restored between the two families and Billy agrees to wait for the money. Jonathan proposes to Cheryl but she leaves him for good. After a long absence, a drunken Sammy visits Owen in hospital. A nurse calls Chrissy to have her removed. Babysitting for the Chois, Sammy helps herself to the drinks cabinet. She gets in a row with Alison, who is a scientist, over animal rights and paint-sprays the word 'murderer' over the side of her car.

Sheila Grant shows off daughter Claire.

BIRTHS

SEPTEMBER

Daniel Sullivan

THE STORY SO FAR
1990

DEATHS

APRIL

James Markham

Sheila Grant helps Kathy Roach (Noreen Kershaw) come to terms with army deserter son Sean (Derek Hicks).

JANUARY

Sinbad is heartbroken when he sees how close Caroline is to her smarmy ex-boyfriend James Markham. Barry and Tracy spend the night together. Billy accuses her of getting back at him because he refused to take Doreen back. Tracy moves out. Sheila has a hard time at the Deaf School. Frank Rogers joins a workers' co-operative to put together a tender for a maintenance contract. At the same time, he is told he is in line for the job of Assistant Transport Manager. To ease her guilt, Sue tells Terry she wants another baby but her plans are postponed when little Danny is rushed to hospital with suspected meningitis.

FEBRUARY

Kathy's soldier son Sean Roach has arrived on the Close. The atmosphere at the Corkhills' becomes even more tense as Sean attacks Sheila and knocks out Barry. He is an army deserter and highly dangerous. Eventually, Kathy takes Sheila's advice and turns him in.

Rumours are rife about a proposed parade of shops near the Close. Harry, Paul and Chrissy are united in their opposition. The co-op win the tender at NCT and Frank is also offered the Assistant Transport Manager's job. Left in a dilemma, Frank feels he owes it to the men and so he turns down the desk job. Danny Sullivan is released from hospital. A stranger, Susan Morgan, confronts Sheila. She says she's Bobby's girlfriend and that she's pregnant. She wants Sheila to agree to a divorce.

MARCH

Sheila discovers that Bobby has had his vasectomy reversed. Now he wants joint custody of Claire. Sheila is devastated and confused and tells Billy she doesn't want to marry him. Trying to solve Sammy's drinking problems, Chrissy strikes up a good rapport with the sympathetic Dr. O'Rourke. It leads to further conflict with Frank. Owen turns up at the Close in a wheelchair. With Harry in Las Vegas for Ralph and Lana's wedding, Mick Johnson moves back into the bungalow. His children Leo and Gemma come to visit. There is a near tragedy when Gemma falls into the goldfish pond — only the swift thinking of Geoff Rogers saves her life. Caroline Choi uncovers a fraud in her jewellery business and eventually realises that James, deep in debt, is responsible.

APRIL

On the run from his shady business associates, James Markham is killed in a car crash in Aberdeen. The police suspect he was murdered. Caroline leaves the Close and Michael and Alison are America-bound. Chrissy embarks on an affair

with Joe O'Rourke. Tracy has a new customer — a young admirer named Liam Riley. Sue and Terry are alarmed to hear that Jonathan is putting the house up for sale so that he can buy out his partner Sarah. Sheila's torment continues until, about to leave Billy, she appreciates that she has too much to lose. She agrees to marry him.

MAY

Sue sinks into depression when she discovers that, despite planning the timing of her lovemaking with Terry with military precision, she's still not pregnant. The recently-returned Lucy Collins spectacularly fails to hit it off with Louise, who tries to impress her by telling her about Annabelle's affair. Paul feels betrayed. Michael and Alison depart for Boston, Massachusetts, and Sinbad moves into the Chois as official caretaker. Liam continues to pester Tracy and declares his love for her. At the salon, he presents her with an engraved bracelet and tries to kiss her, but Barry intervenes and throws him out. In an attempt to put Liam off, Tracy tells him the truth — that she is pregnant. Liam commits suicide by throwing himself from a building.

JUNE

The Collinses move to the Lake District. Lucy leaves to manage a restaurant in France while Gordon considers a business venture with his new-found friend Judith. Tracy packs her bags and, despite Barry's pleas, has an abortion. When she returns, she finishes with Barry. In The Swan, Jimmy attacks Joey Godden, the thug who years earlier had murdered Billy and Jimmy's brother, Frankie. Jimmy vows to

avenge Frankie's death. Frank Rogers packs in the co-op but his boss, Marsland, refuses to give him his job back. Terry decides to take a sperm test and is furious when he gets the results.

JULY

Terry now knows he cannot have children and demands to know who Danny's father is. He throws Sue out and attempts to destroy all evidence of her and Danny's presence in the house. Barry maliciously tells him that Jonathan must be the real father but Jonathan, under duress, reveals that it's Martin Howes. Sue says Martin knows nothing about the baby and that she still wants to be with Terry but he responds by snatching Danny. Jimmy ends up in hospital after tangling with Godden and Sheila tells Billy that Barry is not Bobby's son.

Billy and Jimmy Corkhill are tired of waiting at the end of the cue to talk to Joey Godden.

THE STORY SO FAR
1990

Even the cake was in tiers – an emotional moment as Billy marries Sheila.

SEPTEMBER

Barry plans a warehouse party but Terry, realising it is illegal, wants nothing to do with it. Now living in St. Helens, Harry Cross decides to let the bungalow to Mick on a long-term basis. Josie and the children move back in. To the dismay of her kids, Chrissy Rogers obtains a job as the school secretary. The Corkhills' cousin Don is killed in a pub brawl with Godden. Then Frankie's tombstone is delivered through their front door. Sheila, Billy and Claire drive off to make a fresh start in Basingstoke, leaving Barry, armed with a shotgun, to put the fear of God into Godden. Amidst the mayhem, the Farnhams move into 7 Brookside Close but their hopes of a peaceful existence are swiftly shattered by the backfiring of their new neighbours' van.

OCTOBER

The Dixons achieve the impossible — they manage to lower the tone of Brookside Close. It is instant war with the Farnhams whose nanny Margaret gets into trouble for allowing Ron Dixon to park the Moby on her employers' drive. Owen is furious at the way Sammy flirts with Mike Dixon. Sammy finishes with Owen. Frank gets a job as a lorry driver, while Leo Johnson runs away from school after suffering racial abuse. Tracy and her pal Nikki head for Rhodes, where they both enjoy holiday romances. Sue's mother dies and Terry finds himself comforting Sue. He asks her and Danny to come back and puts the divorce on hold. Jonathan is moving to London and offers to sell the house to Terry and Sue for £40,000. They have just six weeks in which to raise the deposit.

AUGUST

As the wedding draws near, Jimmy takes delivery of a wreath from Godden bearing the message 'Billy and Sheila – R.I.P.' After a last-minute hitch when Billy's taxi fails to arrive, he and Sheila are married. Billy goes to make his peace with Godden but, driving away, Godden tries to run him over. A scared Billy reveals his criminal past to Rod and asks him to 'unofficially' deter Godden. The Collinses' garden shed in which Sinbad is reduced to sleeping catches fire but Sinbad survives. Mick's estranged wife Josie briefly moves in with him after splitting up with her boyfriend Tony. Frank gets a job as Assistant Transport Manager with LICHEM, only to be sacked for unsatisfactory references. Terry files for divorce.

THE STORY SO FAR
1990

NOVEMBER

Tracy is sacked from the salon when Antony learns that she has been touting for business from the regular clientele. Tracy sets up at home. The Rogers fall out over the conflict between Geoff's education and his football career. Mick is beaten up in his taxi and, despite his opposition, Josie gets a part-time job at the notorious Fourstar Club. While working undercover at a supermarket, Rod is flattered by the attentions of Diana, a pharmacy attendant who served him with spot cream. At school, Mike Dixon attacks a sixth-form boy, Sinnott, whom he sees talking to his sister Jackie. Mike is suspended.

DECEMBER

The truth emerges about Mike's feud — Sinnott once gave Jackie some acid at a party and Mike found her sick and frightened by the experience. Rod and his colleague Tommo investigate dog fighting but Rod lies about his job to Diana. Barry offers to lend Terry and Sue the £4,000 for the deposit on the mortgage. After much agonising, they accept. Barry double crosses his financial backers at a warehouse party and runs off with their cut. Thinking Sue is Barry's wife, they kidnap her and Danny. Barry negotiates their release and is dumped inside a meat freezer. Mick catches a burglar trying to break into the children's bedroom and renders him unconscious. Mick feels his actions were totally justifiable and cannot believe it when he learns that the intruder plans to prosecute him for 'undue force.' Can't a man protect his family and property?

Mike Dixon (Paul Byatt) tells Sinnott to keep away from sister Jackie.

THE STORY SO FAR
1991

JANUARY

Rod and Tommo successfully bust the dog fight and Rod is finally able to tell Diana that he's not really a trainee supermarket manager. Diana is not amused at the deception. The police catch Mike and Jackie Dixon in possession of drugs. Mike gets his revenge on Sinnott by spiking his cola — an act that results in Sinnott throwing himself through a window. Sammy returns from a hotel management course with a mystery new man in her life. Ron Dixon puts his name down for one of the new shops near the Close. Faced with Josie's catalogue of debts, poor Mick is also charged with assault.

FEBRUARY

Terry and Sue legally become home owners and Terry plants a tree to mark the occasion. Mike and Jackie escape with a caution over the drugs offence. When Rod is attacked in a pub, Tracy meets his handsome workmate Mark. Frank is stunned to see Sammy kissing her taxi driver and then realises, to his horror, that this man in his late thirties is her secret new boyfriend Tim Derby. Chrissy tells her old friend Gina about her near affair with Dr. O'Rourke and fears that Sammy will make the same mistake as she did and settle down to marriage too soon. But, flying in the face of parental disapproval, Sammy agrees to join Tim on a week's course in Nottingham. Against his solicitor's advice, Mick elects for trial by jury.

MARCH

Barry asks Tracy out but she tells him she is dating Mark. Geoff Rogers is going out with Paula Heneghen despite being warned off by her father. Terry and Sue visit a consultant who tells them that it could be possible for them to have another child. There is open hostility between Barry and Sue and full-scale warfare at the Rogers' where Sammy's relationship with Tim is causing Frank and Chrissy bitterly to re-examine their past. Katie Rogers overhears that her Mum had to get married because she was pregnant. Sammy leaves home and moves in with Tim. Frank storms round to the hotel and demands his daughter back. He warns Tim that if he breaks Sammy's heart, he'll break him!

APRIL

The cabbies have rallied round with a collection to support Mick but Josie 'borrows' the cash to buy children's clothes from Jimmy for her new market stall. Mick is found not guilty but he blows his top when he discovers that Josie has taken the cab money. Max realises his job with the Electricity Board is a mistake and hands in his notice. While Patricia is polishing up her advertising campaign for Kleen-Sheen, Max presents her with a new kitchen. When a council lorry arrives to shift Max's old kitchen units, he gets them to take away some of the Dixons' property too. Ron and Max end up in an unseemly scuffle. In revenge, Ron builds a wall of garish old doors between his house and the Farnhams'. It is the great *Brookside* divide.

MAY

Nikki and Tommo move into the Corkhills', and Rod and Diana contemplate getting engaged. Barry and Mark Potter enter a personal vendetta over Tracy. Patricia is offered a job in London. Max tries to dissuade her from taking it. Patricia is angered by his selfish attitude and accepts it on a month's trial. Sammy invites Chrissy and Frank round to Tim's for a meal. Predictably, it ends in a slanging match. After an awkward dinner with Tim's children, Chloe and Adam, Sammy is shocked to learn that Tim has to go away for three weeks. Geoff Rogers is rejected by Tranmere Rovers. Terry's test results confirm that he is now fertile but he is stunned when Sue, enjoying life at work, changes her mind and says she wants to wait before having another baby.

JUNE

Mark tries to rape Tracy who, in self defence, stabs him in the arm with a pair of hairdressing scissors. In the station locker room, Rod tells Mark to get out of the force. Mark applies for a transfer. A disillusioned Geoff walks out of his exams. Mike Dixon challenges Sinnott to a daredevil car race. Tim finishes with Sammy and tells her to 'go home to daddy'. But Sammy refuses to accept that the relationship is over, even when Tim throws her out. She goes back to his house and makes a scene on the doorstep, only to receive the cold water treatment — all over her head. She responds by throwing a brick through his window.

JULY

Injured in the car race, Mike is taken to hospital. Patricia has to decide whether to accept the London job on a permanent basis. Max finally gets a job through his Round Table contacts and rushes down to London to tell Patricia who rejects the post when she hears his good news. Geoff's soccer career is resurrected when he gets a YTS placement with Torquay United. Sammy tries to win back Owen. Margaret

Sammy used to like a drink — and well tanked-up, she comes between Owen and his girlfriend Grace.

THE STORY SO FAR
1991

Terry Sullivan gets a graveside grip on Graeme Curtis.

O'Rourke. Frank tells Chrissy to leave. To mark their wedding anniversary, Sue and Terry have a major row about her not wanting another baby. Terry smashes all the plates and storms out of the house. Barry comes round to comfort her and they end up having sex. Jimmy, moving into the big-league, is get-away driver on a night club raid. One of his accomplices turns out to be Joey Godden. As Godden races to the car to make his escape after the robbery, Jimmy locks the door and drives off, leaving Godden to be shot by one of the bouncers.

SEPTEMBER
Lying low, Jimmy goes round to talk to his ex-wife Jackie. Chrissy and Katie return to Frank in an uneasy peace. And Sinbad has found a friend at last — Josie's mate Marcia. Derek tells Margaret that their friendship is dangerous and Patricia is fretting over the frequent appearances of Susannah, which are making her feel more and more left out. While Fran fancies Barry, Graeme becomes increasingly obsessed with Sue. He steals a scarf and a family photo from Sue's desk. Fran later discovers the photo in Graeme's desk — with Terry and Danny cut out.

OCTOBER
Jackie Dixon wants an expensive pair of trainers. Sue tells Graeme that unless he stops pestering her, she'll report him to the firm's senior partners. She takes a day off work but Graeme brings her flowers, saying he must talk to her. Individually, Barry and Terry see Sue talking to Graeme outside the shops. While her back is turned, Danny climbs to the top of the scaffolding. Sue climbs up to rescue him.

and her friend Derek, DD's priest brother, take down Ron's makeshift wall. Julia has got her hooks into Ron's Dad, Cyril, but finds out that he's a bigamist. After work, Sue goes for a drink with her colleague Fran but finds herself left alone with Graeme Curtis, who is clearly attracted to her.

AUGUST
Racist Ron disapproves of Jackie's new boyfriend Keith Rooney while Diana's father takes an instant dis-like to Rod being a policeman. Mick's trouble-making brother Ellis turns up and, equally suddenly, Josie walks out on Mick and the kids and goes back to Tony. Drifting ever further apart, Chrissy and Frank start an argument which ends in her telling him about Dr.

Someone else is up there too. The next thing, Sue and Danny plunge to their deaths. Unable to account for his movements, Terry is taken in for questioning, where he is told that Sue was pregnant. What's more, he was the father. When Graeme turns up at the funeral, the police have to drag Terry off him. Graeme is charged with the murders. Elsewhere, Ron opens The Trading Post and Sammy tells Owen that she, too, is pregnant. They decide to marry.

NOVEMBER

Frank is delighted by the news but Chrissy is appalled. She intends leaving the school and the Close for a place at teacher training college. Sure enough, at the wedding reception, Chrissy leaves home for good. Diana reveals that she is illiterate. Rod is unofficially spending a lot of time at an amusement arcade where he was once on undercover surveillance. He talks to a young boy,

Craig, and eventually realises that the lad is a rent boy. Fran tells Barry she knows he slept with Sue. What would Terry think? Ron has got Julia and Jackie Corkhill working in his shop. Mike, heavily in debt, helps himself to cash from the till.

DECEMBER

Rod rather spoils his wedding day by getting beaten up in the toilets at Lime Street Station while trying to rescue Craig from the clutches of his pimp. Diana is left standing at the altar. Rod is suspended from the force. Patricia is worried about a lump on her breast and by the fact that while she was away in London, Susannah spent the night with Max. Max desperately pleads his innocence but Patricia throws him out. Max is devastated. Margaret and Derek declare their love for each other. The Harrisons move into number 9 and Ron discovers Cyril's body. He has had a massive heart attack.

A traumatic moment as Chrissy Rogers (Eithne Browne) walks out on daughter Sammy's wedding day.

THE STORY SO FAR
1992

DEATHS

JANUARY

Graeme Curtis

JANUARY

Ron sacks Julia for stealing from the till. But when Cyril's medals go missing too, he realises that the real thief is his own son. DD Dixon tries to break up Margaret and Derek, and succeeds in getting Derek posted to a parish in the Lake District. At Marcia's suggestion, Sinbad starts to trace his real family. Patricia wants Max back and tells him that she's got breast cancer. She undergoes an operation. A bitter Fran confronts Barry over his interest in Angela, owner of the new hairdressing salon, and threatens to reveal all about him and Sue at Graeme's trial. Graeme is found guilty and is later found dead. At church, Barry confesses to a priest — he was responsible for the deaths of Sue and Danny. Fran tells Terry that Barry slept with Sue. Terry goes at him with a knife.

FEBRUARY

Trying to wreck the reconciliation between Jimmy and Jackie, Jimmy Junior tells her that, years ago, he caught Jimmy in bed with Jackie's sister, Val. But Jimmy's charm wins the day. Sinbad tracks down his long-lost mother and plans to gain a wife, Marcia. Barry forces Fran to say that she was lying about him and Sue. Fran quits Liverpool and

Far from taking part in the Olympic weightlifting, the hapless Graeme Curtis (David Banks) stands in court accused of the murder of Sue and Daniel Sullivan.

Terry decides to open a pizza parlour in Barry's parade of shops. Josie's grandparents turn up and take Leo and Gemma home to Cardiff without asking Mick. The Harrisons suddenly find that they are under investigation for fraud. And the arrival of their son Peter with a wad of cash confirms that John's brother Hugh is at the root of it all.

MARCH

The Harrisons owe Customs and Excise £70,000 and John is forced to shop Hugh to save his own skin. A teenage gang caught thieving from the school by Barbara hurl a brick through the Harrisons' conservatory. They then mug Julia. Katie's schoolfriend Leanne has a crush on Owen. He rejects her blatant advances but she claims he made love to her. It is left to Barbara Harrison to uncover the truth. After briefly walking out on Sammy, Owen returns and gets a job in Terry's pizza parlour. Margaret's Mum is horrified to learn that her daughter is dating a priest. She vows to stop the relationship at all costs.

Jackie Dixon (Alexandra Fletcher) falls for gang - leader Darren Murphy (Matthew Crompton).

comes back to tell Barry she's pregnant — with his child. Frank meets a woman called Denise at a singles' club but an upset Katie sees her as a replacement for Chrissy. And when Margaret attempts to seduce Derek, it all ends in tears.

APRIL

Jackie Dixon goes out with Darren, a member of the gang. They break into a classroom at Manor Park Primary School and Darren starts a fire. Jackie is trapped in the room, only to be rescued by the passing Barry. After Ron tries to nail Darren, a stolen car is driven into the Close and dumped outside the Dixons'. Then Ron's shop window is smashed. Angie's estranged husband Colin wants her back and also wants Barry out of her life. Fran

MAY

Derek goes missing and attempts suicide. Ron, DD and Margaret discover him in the nick of time, in Mike's flat. Derek decides to leave the church. The pizza parlour is closed down by the health department on the grounds of food poisoning. Barry learns that Matty is his real father and then, discovering that the mysterious Asians who have been renting the flat above one of his shops have been printing counterfeit money, proceeds to steal

THE STORY SO FAR
1992

Barry is told who his real father is.

£35,000 of their fake notes. Increasingly desperate, Barry kidnaps Fran and takes her to a lonely beach. He then tells Terry that he killed Sue and Danny. He hands Terry a gun and says that Terry must decide how to carry out justice.

JUNE

With Barry missing presumed dead, it looks as if Terry is to be charged with murder. But Barry turns up and Terry is freed. Sammy's baby is born prematurely and is at death's door while Sinbad and Marcia row after he learns that she can't have children. Mick loses his taxi when Ellis is prosecuted for illegally driving the cab and Jimmy squats in one of the shops. Margaret and Derek go away for the weekend but the lorry

driver friend of Frank's who is taking them suffers a heart attack on the journey and dies. Derek administers the last rites and Margaret realises that, even though he has left the church, he will somehow always be a priest.

JULY

Margaret and Derek have sex at the Farnhams'. Max is furious that she neglected Thomas. Margaret and Derek leave and Max brings in a new nanny, Anna Wolka. DD, livid at Ron's involvement in the Margaret and Derek affair, packs her bags and leaves him for a week. Terry sub-lets the re-opened pizza parlour to Ellis, Frank ditches Denise in favour of new girlfriend Lyn, and Rod and Diana are mar-

BIRTHS

JUNE

Louise Daniels

WEDDINGS

JULY

Rod & Diana Corkhill

THE STORY SO FAR

are reconciled but John Harrison, still pained by early retirement, is arrested for shoplifting. Ron Dixon tries to make amends to DD by planning a big day out for their twentieth wedding anniversary. A gang of armed raiders also have plans — to snatch the wages from Angela Lambert's hair salon. They burst in while Diana is having her hair done. Rod, who has come to collect her, attempts to stop the raid and has his face slashed with a knife for his pains. The aftermath of the raid is felt throughout the community — and has made Diana even more convinced that Rod must leave the police. After all, it's his second injury within the call of duty. Frank and Lyn prepare to go camping with the Dixons in Scotland. Proud parents Ron and DD decide to make a surprise trip for the screening of Mike's film at the Young People's Television Festival.

SEPTEMBER

A traumatised Angela quits the salon. Rod packs in his job. Meanwhile, Diana — whose confidence has been growing since attending illiteracy classes — is becoming less dependent on him and gets a new job in Manchester. Patricia Farnham is pregnant, and Margaret and Derek celebrate their engagement. Jackie Dixon has dropped the bombshell to her parents that she wants to leave school and start work at the leisure centre. Brian Kennedy, the salon's new franchise owner, asks Tracy to be the mangeress. Marianne Dwyer dates Ellis, but Mick also seems keen on her. Rod goes for a job interview as a security officer, and Barbara Harrison applies for a job in Cheshire.

ried at last — at a register office. They return to the Close, where the Corkhill clan has gathered for a surprise wedding reception. Sammy rejects her new baby, Louise, and leaves her outside a hospital and walks away. Louise is taken into care before Owen gets her back and takes her to his Mum's — where he knows she'll be safe – away from Sammy.

AUGUST

Sammy, Owen and Louise are reunited and think about getting a place of their own. Patricia packs in her job and goes solo as a public relations consultant and, in a bid to buy the pizza parlour off Terry, Ellis goes to a loan shark. Terry is going downhill fast. Sinbad and Marcia

8 ROLL CALL

Brookside *creator and executive producer Phil Redmond turns the* Close *into a seat of learning after being made an Honorary Professor of Media Studies.*

Character	Actor
Marcia Barrett	Cheryl Maiker
Nisha Batra	Sunetra Sarker
Heather Black (née Haversham)	Amanda Burton
Nicholas Black	Alan Rothwell
Cheryl Boyanowsky	Jennifer Calvert
Julia Brogan	Gladys Ambrose
Ducksie Brown	Mark Birch
Kirsty Brown	Joanne Black
Mark Callaghan	Dean Williams
Caroline Choi	Sarah Lam
Jessica Choi	Anna Sung
Michael Choi	David Yip
John Clarke	Robert Pugh
Vicki Cleary	Cheryl Leigh
Margaret Clemence	Nicola Stephenson
Annabelle Collins	Doreen Sloane
Gordon Collins	Nigel Crowley / Mark Burgess
Lucy Collins	Katrin Cartlidge / Maggie Saunders / Katrin Cartlidge (again)
Paul Collins	Jim Wiggins
Billy Corkhill	John McArdle
Diana Corkhill (née Spence)	Paula Frances
Doreen Corkhill	Kate Fitzgerald
Jackie Corkhill	Sue Jenkins
Jimmy Corkhill	Dean Sullivan
Rod Corkhill	Jason Hope
Sheila Corkhill (née Grant)	Sue Johnston
Tracy Corkhill	Justine Kerrigan
Lana Costello	Diana Ricardo
Craig	Paul McNulty
Edna Cross	Betty Alberge
Harry Cross	Bill Dean
Graeme Curtis	David Banks
Tom Curzon	Brian Stephens
Owen Daniels	Danny McCall
Sammy Daniels (née Rogers)	Rachael Lindsay
Charlie Dawson	Philip McGough
Tim Derby	Christopher Blake
Cyril Dixon	Allan Surtees
DD Dixon	Irene Marot
Jackie Dixon	Alexandra Fletcher
Mike Dixon	Paul Byatt
Ron Dixon	Vince Earl
Tony Dixon	Gerard Bostock
	Mark Lennock
Christopher Duncan	Stifyn Parri
Gerald Fallon	Bryan Matheson
Mona Fallon (née Harvey)	Margaret Clifton
Max Farnham	Steven Pinder
Patricia Farnham	Gabrielle Glaister
Susannah Farnham	Karen Drury
Joey Godden	Carl Chase
Jonathan Gordon-Davies	Steven Pinner
Laura Gordon-Davies (née Wright)	Jane Cunliffe
Barry Grant	Paul Usher
Bobby Grant	Ricky Tomlinson
Damon Grant	Simon O'Brien
Karen Grant	Shelagh O'Hara
Alison Gregory	Alyson Spiro
Pat Hancock	David Easter
Ralph Hardwick	Ray Dunbobbin
Barbara Harrison	Angela Morant
John Harrison	Geoffrey Leesley
Peter Harrison	Robert Beck
Gizzmo Hawkins	Robert Smith
Sally Haynes	Roberta Kerr
Jamie Henderson	Sean McKee
Brian 'Bumper' Humphries	James Mawdsley
Roger Huntington	Rob Spendlove
Dr. Tony Hurrell	Martin Wenner
Gary Jackson	Allan Patterson
George Jackson	Cliff Howells
Little George Jackson	Steven Patterson
Marie Jackson	Anna Keaveney
Ellis Johnson	Francis Johnson
Gemma Johnson	Naomi Kamanga
Josie Johnson	Suzanne Packer
Leo Johnson	Leeon Sawyer
Mick Johnson	Louis Emerick
Alun Jones	Norman Eshley
Michelle Jones	Tracey Jay
Angela Lambert	Hilary Welles
Brian Lawrence	Vincent Maguire
Sandra Maghie	Sheila Grier
James Markham	Tom Mannion
Mrs. McArdle	Peggy Shields
Tommy McArdle	Malcolm Tierney
Debbie McGrath	Gillian Kearney
Kate Moses	Sharon Rosita
Matty Nolan	Tony Scoggo
Teresa Nolan	Ann Haydn Edwards
Derek O'Farrell	Clive Moore
Dr. O'Rourke	Christian Rodska
Andrea Parkin	Jane Morant
Alan Partridge	Dicken Ashworth
Samantha Partridge	Dinah May
Fran Pearson	Julie Peasgood
Mark Potter	Paul Crosby
Leanne Powell	Vickie Gates
Madge Richmond	Shirley Stelfox
Shelley Rimmer	Lesley Nicol
Kathy Roach	Noreen Kershaw
Sean Roach	Derek Hicks
Chrissy Rogers	Eithne Browne
Frank Rogers	Peter Christian
Geoff Rogers	Kevin Carson
Katie Rogers	Debbie Reynolds
	Diane Burke
Keith Rooney	Kirk Smith
Richard de Saville	Robert Dallas
Sinbad	Michael Starke
Sizzler	Renny Krupinski
Mike Stevens	Saul Jephcott
Jack Sullivan	William Maxwell
Sue Sullivan (née Harper)	Annie Miles
Terry Sullivan	Brian Regan
Ruth Sweeney	Mary Healey
Gavin Taylor	Daniel Webb
Petra Taylor	Alexandra Pigg
Tommo	John O'Gorman
Nikki White	Michelle Byatt
Ronnie Williams	Claire Robinson

Abraham, Michele
Allison, Romey
Andrew, Dorothy
Andrew, Paul
Andrews, Helen
Armitage, Kim
Backhouse, Rodney
Baldwin, Honora
Beresford, Martin
Bimson, David
Black, Helen
Blagden, Sandra
Blake, Darrol
Blanthorn, Timothy
Boisseau, Peter
Boundy, Elaine
Bowman, Mev
Boyd, Frank
Boyes, Candida
Brannigan, Sheila
Brookes, Gareth
Brookfield, Kevin
Brown, Graham
Buck, Ruth
Burdett, Julie
Burnett, Liz
Butterworth, Sue
Byrne, Roy
Byrne, Stephen
Cain, Alex
Cain, Janetta
Cain, Pauline
Carlton, Bob
Carrington, Brian
Carroll, Stephen
Carson, Anthony
Carter, James
Caulfield, Alex
Cavacuiti, Peter
Caveen, Tony
Chapman, Greg
Christopher, Pauline
Clark, Anne
Clough, Chris
Coles, Susan
Corrie, Andrew
Cotton, Paul
Crampton, Barbara
Craven, Diane
Dacey, Anna
Dastoor, Julia
Davie, Linda
Davies, Peter
Davitt, Michelle
Dean, Jean
Deaves, Graham
Desmond, Gary
Donat, Julia
Donnelly, Kim
Doran, Mark
Dorr, Sandra
Doughty, Stuart
Duff, Erica
Duncan, Ian
Duncan, Ian
Duncan, Lorraine
Dunn, Susan
Dyson, Denise
Ealey, Maureen
Edwards, Josephine
Egerton, Graham

Evans, Keith
Farley, Rona
Fealey, David
Fearon, Peter
Feeney, Deborah
Felmingham, Pat
Folkard, John
Foster, Henry
Fowler, Susan
Fraser, Ian
Fraser, Mary
Freeman, Janet
Fywell, Tim
Gabriel, Robert
Gill, Jane
Glazier, Peter
Glover, Alan
Goddard, Duncan
Goddard, Janet
Gould, Jenny
Gowing, Emma
Gowing, Len
Gray, Terence
Green, Terence
Greenidge, Mike
Greenwood, Colette
Griffin, Helen
Griffiths, Stephen
Guiver, Paul
Gupta, Anita
Hambly, Jane
Hanley, Geraldine
Hanna, Elizabeth
Hansen, Julie
Harcombe, Francis
Harper, Stephen
Healey, Geoff
Henderson, Liz
Hendrick, Linda
Henry, Brian
Herdman, Paul
Higgens, Nicky
Higgs, Andrew
Hill, Diana
Hill, Gordon
Hill, Ian Rowland
Hiller, Danny
Hinchley, Ivan
Hocknell, Kate
Hollis, Nancy
Holmes, Sandie
Horan, Mike
Horn, Ken
Horn, Linda
Howard, Karen
Howells, Viv
Hutchman, David
Ion, Gill
Jennings, Moira
Johnson, Jo
Johnston, Chris
Johnston, Ida
Johnston, Peter
Jones, David
Jones, Karen
Jones, Neil
Kan, Garie
Kelly, Rita
Kerr, Paul
Kerrigan, Paul
Kewley, Paula

King, Peter
Kirkham, David
Klinger, Billie
Lally, Jenny
Latta, Brian
Laughland, Nick
Laurie, Joan
Leach, Philip
Leigh, Elizabeth
Leighton, Jane
Lenton, Susanna
Leonard, Amanda
Letts, Barry
Lighthill, Brian
Lines, Kevin
Lister, Paul
Lloyd, David
Lodmore, Michael
Long, Jacqueline
Lovett, Chris
Lovgreen, Chris
Lynch, Imelda
Lynn, Riitta
Maddox, Vinny
Magee, Maggie
Maguire, Ged
Malone, Leigh
Maloney, Carmel
Malpas, Liz
Mansell, Barbara
Marray, Brigid
Marsden, Alan
Martin, Joanne
Mathews, Dot
May, Lisa
Mears, Dawn
Mercer, Billy
Mocroft, Angela
Morgan, Brian
Morgan, Sally
Morris, Anthony
Moseley, Brenda
Mottershead, Wayne
Mulhearn, James
Murphy, David
Murphy, Dennis
Murphy, Teri
Musker, Dianne
Mutch, Debra
MacDonald, Bruce
McCann, Nick
McCarthy, Karen
McCormick, John
McCracken, John
McDonough, Terry
McDowell, Kenneth
McGinn, Patricia
McGrath, David
McGregor, Alex
McKeown, Colin
McLoughlin, Lilian
McNabb, John
McQuoid, Mark
McVerry, Janet
Naylor, Jeff
Neill, Richie
Nelson, Brian
Nordin, Eszter
Nugent, Julie
Oakley, Douglas
Orchard, Nick

Overton, Dale
Owen, Derek
Owens, Trevor
Parker, John
Paton, Jenny
Patrick, Kay
Patterson, Charlie
Pilkington, Gloria
Player, Piers
Povey, Joan
Prosser, Nick
Quayle, Sandra
Quinn, Anthony
Quinn, Simon
Rabette, Marie
Redmond, Alexis
Redmond, Larry
Reevell, Philip
Regan, Lisa
Relph, Colin
Reynolds, Thalia
Riches, Sarah
Ridley, Sally
Roddick, Carolyn
Rohrer, Rob
Rooney, Jackie
Roper, Frances
Rowlands, Norman
Royle, Christopher
Rushton, Joanne
Russell, Graham
Ryan, Sue
Sarony, Paul
Seiga, Margaret
Senn, Sharon
Severs, Anthony
Shaw, Jennifer
Sheeran, Carol
Simpson, Bren
Sinclair, Maureen
Skinner, Susan
Sless, Simone
Smiley, Jan
Smith, Arthur
Smith, David
Smith, Donna
Smith, Helen
Smith, Julia
Sorenson, Jon
Spence, Richard
Spenton-Foster, George
Standeven, Richard
Stanton, Linda
Stephenson, Rachel
Stewart, Rod
Strawson, Vincent
Strickland, John
Stuart, Rob
Swain, Jonathon
Sweeney, Terry
Tattan, Jayne
Taylor, Paul
Tempia, Martin
Thomas, Cheryl
Thomson, Archie
Thornton, Darrell
Titchen, Richard
Trafford, Paula
Troup, Janice
Tucker, Garth
Tucker, Patrick

Vasey, Ian
Walmsey, Madeleine
Walters, Anthony
Ward, Julie
Washington, Keith
Waters, Mark
Watling, Mick
Watson, Hugh
Webster, Lauren
Weston, Ian
Whitburn, Vanessa
White, Ann-Marie
Wileman, Robert
Williams, Gary
Williams, Helen
Williams, Katherine
Williams, Lynn
Williams, Misha
Wilson, Jane
Winslade, Dennis
Wood, Anne
Wood, Karen
Wood, Tony
Wooding, Jenny
Wright, Anne
Wright, Robert
Wright, Steve
Young, Mal

Brookside Writers Past And Present

Ainsworth, Joe
Angus, David
Bernard, Chris
Bessman, Maurice
Boyle, Joe
Clarke, Frank
Cottrell Boyce, Frank
Cox, Peter
Curry, Chris
Duggan, Shaun
Godber, John
Goddard, Janet
Hayes, Catherine
Hitchmough, Jim
Jacobs, Sam
Lynch, Andy
MacDonald, Alan
McGovern, Jimmy
Mellor, Kay
Needle, Jan
Oakden, John
Oakes, Jimmy
Parisella, Mina
Pleat, Susan
Potter, Kathleen
Redmond, Phil
Rush, Len
Swift, Allan
Wilson, Helen
Windsor, Valerie
Woodward, Barry

A GREAT TEAM EFFORT

BOXTREE/BROOKSIDE QUIZ

NOW YOU'VE WATCHED THE SERIAL... AND READ THE BOOK... DO THE QUIZ –
and find out just how well you really know the characters on Brookside Close!

This is your chance to win a Sony Camcorder and record your day out on the *Brookside* set. You and a friend will get the chance to visit the Close, the Shopping Parade, and meet Barry, Terry, and all your favourite Brookside stars— and the whole fabulous day will be recorded on your Sony Camcorder for posterity!

All you have to do is answer these 4 easy questions—easy if you're a *Brookside* fan, of course!

1 Paul Byatt isn't the only member of the Byatt family to appear in Brookside. Name the others and the roles they play or have played?

2 Which social event involving the rest of the Close's characters gave Sammy and Owen the opportunity to slip away and make love on the Sullivans' sofa?

3 What is Sinbad's real name in full?

4 What was Executive Producer Phil Redmond's very first job?

All entries should be submitted on a postcard no later than
31 January 1993 to: Boxtree Ltd
21 Broadwall
London SE1 9PL

RULES